JAMES McNAIR's
CUSTARDS, MOUSSES & PUDDINGS

Photography by James McNair

Chronicle Books • San Francisco

Printed in Hong Kong.

Library of Congress
Cataloging-in-Publication Data
McNair, James K.
[Custards, mousses & puddings]
James McNair's custards, mousses & puddings/
photography by James McNair
p. cm.
Includes indexes.
ISBN 0-87701-829-4.
ISBN 0-87701-823-5 (pbk.)
1. Cookery (Puddings)
2. Mousses.
I. Title.
II. Title: James McNair's custards, mousses, and puddings.
TX773.M347 1992
641.8'64—dc20   92-23691
                              CIP

Distributed in Canada by
Raincoast Books
112 East Third Avenue
Vancouver, British Columbia V5T 1C8

10 9 8 7 6 5 4 3 2 1

Chronicle Books
275 Fifth Street
San Francisco, California 94103

For my nephew, Devereux McNair, who has the most sophisticated palate of any child I have ever known and who fills my life with love and laughter.

And in memory of my grandmother Mary Izetta McNair of Baskin, Louisiana, whose banana pudding left an indelible impression in my mind of what good home cooking is all about.

Produced by The Rockpile Press, Napa Valley and Lake Tahoe, California

Art direction, photographic and food styling, and book design by James McNair

Editorial, styling, and photographic assistance by Andrew Moore

Typography and mechanical production by Cleve Gallat of CTA Graphics

CONTENTS

INTRODUCTION

Since custards, mousses, and other puddings are my favorite desserts, it came as a surprise that this book idea proved to be difficult to sell to my publisher. When I initially proposed the title several years ago, their only response was a rendition of the venerable Jell-O jingle accompanied by frowns and remembrances of school lunches and sickbeds. To the group of youthful professionals in charge, the subject of puddings was too passé to qualify for this series of books devoted to what is happening with American food.

But I did not give up. I resubmitted the idea for this book each year, only to be rejected each time. With renewed determination, I requested a meeting with the Chronicle Books editorial board. My assistant and I showed up at mid-afternoon armed with six different puddings. As the board members lapped up every morsel, I hastily pointed out the origin of each concoction. In addition to a New Orleans bread pudding that was still warm from my own oven, the array consisted of puddings that had been picked up that afternoon from celebrated San Francisco restaurants where they were featured on the day's dessert menu. There was silky butterscotch pudding from Bradley Ogden's Lark Creek Inn, a *pot de crème* from the popular Zuni Cafe, trifle from the kitchen of Jeremiah Tower's Stars, and two variations on *crème brûlée*, one from Joyce Goldstein's Square One and the other from the famed Hayes Street Grill. My point was made.

As this tasting proved, puddings in all forms are definitely part of the contemporary American food scene. Even those who turn up their noses at the mention of the word *puddings* are likely to order one, especially when they are called by their fancy European monikers—*crème brûlée,* mousse, *pot de crème, tiramisù,* zabaglione, and so on. In fact, these favored sweets are all puddings.

The term *pudding* comes to us from our English founders, who have long had a reputation as pudding fanciers. George I was dubbed the Pudding King; the richer and sweeter the puddings, the better he liked them.

In the late seventeenth century, when sugar became plentiful and cheap in England, wickedly sweet puddings became popular. This fascination did not last, however. When the fun-loving Puritans came on the scene, they banned puddings because they contained spices that were considered flavorings of the devil. When Charles II assumed the throne, dessert puddings returned in full glory. By the reign of Victoria, puddings had become elaborate works of art, made in molds and embellished with gold and silver leaf. British cooks deserve credit for inventing baked and stirred custards, rice puddings, bread puddings, and steamed puddings.

These wondrous sweets were too good to be confined to the British Isles and quickly spread throughout the world. Although caramel custard *(crème caramel)* and burnt cream *(crème brûlée)* were English in origin, their French names are more common and we think of them as French desserts. On the North American continent, the people of each region took their own food specialties and created such diverse local recipes as persimmon pudding, pumpkin custard, maple mousse, Creole bread pudding, Mexican bread and cheese pudding *(capirotada)*, and Indian pudding, a rich simmered sweet made from cornmeal (see *James McNair's Corn Cookbook* for a recipe).

In England the term *pudding* is synonymous with dessert and covers a wide range of both sweet and savory dishes. In America we have narrowed the group of sweets that we call puddings to include those that are eaten with spoons and have either a custard consistency or are baked cakelike concoctions that maintain a gooey or sticky texture.

I've divided this book into three sections. CUSTARDS includes those smooth, creamy concoctions that are rich in calories and rich with memories of both homey and haute cuisine. MOUSSES contains several variations on the theme of fluffy cloudlike desserts that float across the tongue. PUDDINGS is a section of baked treats that offer comforting thoughts of good home cooking. Here you will find bread pudding, persimmon pudding, and those towering steamed puddings that are too often reserved only for winter holiday tables.

OTHER McNAIR PUDDINGS

There are so many wonderful custards, mousses, and puddings that it was a difficult task to choose which recipes should be included in this little book. Fortunately, I've been able to feature many of my best puddings in other volumes in this single-subject series.

Please don't miss one of my most successful sweets, Summer Berry and Polenta Pudding, in *Cold Cuisine.* A recipe for Jewish Noodle Pudding, or kugel, is in the perennially popular *Cold Pasta.* My *Potato Cookbook* has a delectably icky-sticky Caribbean Sweet Potato-Coconut Loaf, and the Steamed Winter Pudding in the *Squash Cookbook* is worth the price of the volume.

I adore rice pudding and offer my apology for the lack of space to include one or two in this collection. My *Rice Cookbook,* however, features a half dozen international rice puddings.

CUSTARDS

Whether a homey vanilla cup custard that recalls childhood days or an elegantly sophisticated caramel *pot de crème,* custards are among the world's most satisfying desserts. Smooth custards may be made in the oven or on the stove top. The secrets for success are good ingredients and low, steady heat. Eggs are a principal ingredient, and it is essential that they not curdle from heat that is too high at any point during cooking.

Trifle is an eighteenth-century English dessert of custard layered with cake and fruits. Sponge cake or lady fingers are spread with jam, placed in a glass bowl, sprinkled with sherry, and layered with fruit and a rich custard. Probably because the cook was often quite generous with the spirited flavorings, trifles have also been called "tipsy cakes." When English cooks substitute whipped cream for the custard and replace the sherry with brandy, they have made the fancifully named whim-wham.

A Bavarian cream is a French custard that is lightened with whipped cream and/or beaten egg whites and stabilized with gelatin. Bavarians are chilled in a mold until firmly set, then turned out for presentation.

Diplomat pudding is a stirred stove-top custard that is poured inside a container lined with ladyfingers or sponge cake slices, sometimes sandwiched together with jam. American banana pudding is a simpler variation that lines the dish with vanilla wafers. These bakery product-encased desserts are similar to charlottes, except that a charlotte is a Bavarian cream or other gelatin-thickened custard that sets up in a mold, is chilled, and is then unmolded and decorated.

Italian *tiramisù,* which is undergoing a period of enormous popularity in America, is more closely akin to a charlotte than to its Italian ancestor, *zuppa inglese,* a relative of the English trifle. The custardy filling is made from whipped mascarpone cheese enriched with egg yolk.

STORING

I prefer most custards while they are still warm, often making refrigeration unnecessary. Some custards such as *crème brûlée* and those that are molded, such as charlottes, require chilling to set up, however, and their delicate flavors can easily be ruined upon contact with other food odors.

When you must refrigerate custards, wrap tightly in plastic wrap. Eat them as quickly as possible; most are best on the day they are made. Do not keep them for more than 24 hours before serving.

Baked Custard

Basic vanilla custard, also known as cup custard or egg custard, is good plain, either warm or at room temperature, or with warm Caramel Sauce (page 89), Chocolate Sauce (page 89), fresh berries, or sliced fruits. The recipe can be altered in countless ways, however; the next two pages offer more than a dozen variations or you may add your own favorite flavorings. For the photograph, I made the Coffee Custard variation and drizzled the chilled custard with Chocolate Glaze (page 91).

Preheat an oven to 300° F.

In a saucepan, combine the milk, half-and-half, and/or cream and the vanilla bean (if used). Place over medium-low heat and warm the milk mixture until bubbles form along the edges of the pan; do not let it boil. Remove from the heat and let cool slightly.

In a bowl, beat the whole eggs or egg yolks lightly with a fork; avoid overbeating at any point to prevent too many air bubbles from forming. Stir in the sugar and salt. Strain the milk through a fine-mesh sieve into a pitcher, then gradually stir it into the egg mixture until smooth. If using a vanilla bean, scrape the seeds into the mixture; alternatively, stir in the vanilla extract. Strain the mixture into a pitcher and then carefully pour the mixture into a 2-quart baking dish, six eight-ounce ovenproof glass or ceramic custard cups, or eight 6-ounce ovenproof glass or ceramic custard cups. Grate a bit of nutmeg over the top (if used).

Transfer the container(s) to a baking pan, place the pan in the oven, and pour in enough hot (not boiling) water to reach about two thirds of the way up the sides of the container(s). Bake until a knife inserted near the edge of the custard comes out barely clean, about 45 minutes; the center should still wobble slightly when a container is shaken. Regulate oven temperature during baking to maintain water at the almost simmering stage; do not allow to boil. Transfer the custards to a wire rack.

Serve warm or at room temperature, or cover tightly and chill for several hours or overnight.

Makes 6 to 8 servings.

4 cups milk, half-and-half, or heavy (whipping) cream, or a mixture (see sidebar on page 10)
1 vanilla bean, split lengthwise, or 2 teaspoons pure vanilla extract
6 whole eggs, or 8 egg yolks
⅔ cup sugar, or to taste
Pinch of salt
Nutmeg for grating (optional)

BAKED CUSTARD VARIATIONS

OPTIONS

For a richer baked custard or caramel-glazed custard, substitute light cream or half-and-half for the milk. Canned evaporated milk also creates a richer-flavored version. For a super-smooth custard, substitute 1 can (14 ounces) sweetened condensed milk for an equal amount of the milk and omit the sugar. For a tangy flavor, substitute fresh or canned evaporated goat's milk for the cow's milk.

For a lighter baked custard, use low-fat milk, low-fat evaporated milk, or combine two parts low-fat milk with one part freshly squeezed orange juice.

Although *pot de crème* and *crème brûlée* are classicly made only with rich cream, a mixture of half cream and half whole milk appeals to many cooks' tastebuds and waistlines.

For a flavorful surprise, divide about 2 cups chopped or cubed banana, mango, papaya, nectarine, or peach, or whole blueberries or raspberries among the bottoms of the custard cups before pouring in the custard mixture. Or sprinkle about 2 teaspoons shaved or finely chopped good-quality semisweet or bittersweet chocolate in the bottom of each custard dish before adding the custard mixture.

Any one of the following variations may be used when making the preceding recipe for Baked Custard or for Caramel-Glazed Custard on page 12, Pots of Cream *(Pots de Crème)* on page 15, or Burnt Cream *(Crème Brûlée)* on page 16.

Banana Custard. Reduce the milk and/or cream to 3 cups total. Stir 1 cup banana purée, 2 tablespoons light rum, and ½ teaspoon ground cardamom into the completed custard mix. Garnish with sliced banana just before serving.

Cajeta Custard. Reduce the milk and/or cream to 2 cups total. After heating the milk and/or cream, stir in 2 cups heated Caramelized Goat's Milk Sauce *(Cajeta)* on page 89.

Caramel Custard. In a saucepan, combine the sugar with ¼ cup water and stir well. Cover and place over low heat until the sugar dissolves, about 4 minutes. Uncover and cook over medium heat, swirling the pan, until the sugar is a golden amber color. Strain the hot milk and/or cream into a pitcher, then slowly stir it into the sugar mixture until smooth. Now strain the milk mixture into the egg mixture. Except when serving *crème brûlée*, spoon a little warm Caramel Sauce (page 89) over the custards just before serving, if desired.

Carrot Custard. Reduce the milk and/or cream to 3 cups total. Substitute golden brown sugar or maple syrup for the sugar. After heating the milk and/or cream and straining it into the egg mixture, stir in 1 cup puréed carrot and 1 teaspoon ground cinnamon or ginger.

Chocolate Custard. Stir ½ cup unsweetened cocoa powder, preferably Dutch-process type, or to taste, into the sugar before adding it to the eggs. Or chop 6 to 8 ounces good-quality sweetened chocolate (milk, semisweet, or bittersweet) and stir the chocolate into the warming milk and/or cream until melted. Remove from the heat and steep for about 15 minutes before straining.

Citrus Custard. Add the chopped zest of 2 or 3 lemons, limes, oranges, or tangerines to the milk and/or cream before heating. Remove from the heat and steep for about 15 minutes before straining. Except when serving *crème brûlée*, spoon a little warm Lemon Sauce (page 89) over the custards just before serving, if desired.

Coconut Custard. Substitute canned or freshly made coconut milk for all of the milk and/or cream and prepare as directed in basic recipe. Alternatively, substitute 1 can (14 ounces) sweetened condensed milk for an equal amount of the milk and/or cream, omit the sugar, and add 1½ cups freshly grated or unsweetened grated dried coconut to the strained custard. Except when serving *crème brûlée*, sprinkle the custards with a little toasted shredded coconut just before serving, if desired.

Coffee Custard. Stir 2 tablespoons instant-espresso powder or ½ cup cold extra-strong brewed coffee, or to taste, into the heated milk and/or cream. Remove from the heat and steep for about 15 minutes before straining.

Ginger Custard. Add 2 to 3 tablespoons chopped fresh ginger to the milk and/or cream before heating. Remove from the heat and steep for about 15 minutes before straining.

Maple Custard. Substitute pure maple syrup for the sugar in the egg mixture. Except when serving *crème brûlée*, pour a little warm maple syrup over the custards just before serving, if desired.

Mint Custard. Add ½ cup coarsely chopped fresh mint leaves to the milk and/or cream before heating. Remove from the heat and steep for about 15 minutes before straining.

Pumpkin Custard. Reduce the milk and/or cream to 3 cups total. Substitute lightly packed golden brown sugar for the granulated sugar. After adding the strained milk to the egg mixture, stir in 1 cup firmly packed puréed fresh or canned cooked pumpkin (not pumpkin pie filling) or other winter squash, ¼ teaspoon *each* ground cinnamon and freshly grated nutmeg, and ⅛ teaspoon *each* ground allspice and cloves.

Spirited Custard. Add about ¼ cup sherry, brandy, Marsala, port, or other fortified wine or spirit to the strained warm custard mixture.

TOPPINGS

Crumble Glazed Spiced Nuts (page 93) or Praline Topping (page 93) and sprinkle over the tops of any cooled custard just before serving. Or try sprinkling either topping over *crème brûlée* as a crunchy alternative to melted sugar.

Except when serving *crème brûlée*, pipe Chocolate Glaze (page 91) atop cooled custards before serving. Or spoon on a favorite pudding sauce.

Before topping *crème brûlée* with the sugar for melting, sauté thinly sliced apples or pears in butter and arrange atop the chilled custards.

To make crisp sugar toppings for *crème brûlée* several hours ahead of time, cover a baking sheet with aluminum foil. Trace the shape of the bottom of each baking dish onto the foil. Spread on softened butter to cover each circle lightly. Sprinkle a thin layer of sugar evenly over the buttered areas. Place under a preheated broiler until the sugar is melted and caramelized; watch carefully to prevent scorching. Cool completely until the sugar disks harden. Just before serving the custards, lift the sugar disks from the foil with a spatula and slip them over the custard tops.

Caramel-Glazed Custard

1¾ cups sugar
¼ cup water
3 whole eggs
5 egg yolks
2 cans (12 ounces *each*) evaporated
    milk
2 teaspoons pure vanilla extract
Pesticide-free edible flowers such as
    violets for garnish (optional)

The French call this silky concoction *crème caramel;* the Mexicans know it as *flan*. In any language, it is one of my favorite desserts.

Preheat an oven to 350° F. Select a 2-quart metal baking pan, six 8-ounce metal baking containers, or eight 6-ounce metal baking cups.

In a heavy saucepan, combine 1 cup of the sugar and the water and stir well. Place over medium heat, cover, and heat for about 4 minutes. Remove the cover and continue to cook, swirling the pan, until the syrup turns amber, about 8 minutes longer. If sugar crystals begin to form around the sides of the pan just above the bubbling syrup, brush them away with a wet brush. Carefully pour the hot syrup into the reserved pan or cups and quickly swirl the container(s) to coat the bottom and about one third of the way up the sides. Set the container(s) aside to cool.

In a large mixing bowl, combine the whole eggs and egg yolks and beat lightly with a fork; avoid overbeating at any point to prevent too many air bubbles from forming. Stir in the remaining ¾ cup sugar, the milk, and vanilla. Slowly strain the mixture through a fine-mesh sieve into the sugar-lined pan or cups. Cover the container(s) with a lid or aluminum foil and place in a large pan. Pour enough hot water (not boiling) into the pan to reach halfway up the sides of the container(s).

Bake until a knife inserted near the edge of the custard comes out barely clean, about 1 hour for a large container or about 25 minutes for the cups; the center should still wobble slightly when a container is shaken. Regulate oven temperature during baking to maintain water at the almost simmering stage; do not allow to boil. Remove from the hot-water to a countertop and remove lid(s).

To serve warm, let cool for about 15 minutes, then run a thin, sharp knife blade between the custard and the baking dish, cover with an inverted serving plate or individual serving plates, and invert custard(s). Lift off container(s), garnish with flowers (if used), and serve. Caramel syrup will run down the sides and onto the serving dish(es) to surround the custard. Garnish with flowers (if used). Spoon some of the syrup over each portion when serving.

To serve cold, let cool to room temperature, then cover tightly and refrigerate until well chilled, at least 3 hours or as long as overnight. Just before serving, immerse the bottom of the container(s) in a pan of hot water for about 30 seconds and run a thin, sharp knife around the side of the container(s) to loosen the custard. Invert and serve as above.

Makes 6 to 8 servings.

Pots of Cream (Pots de Crème)

This smooth and elegant custard is traditionally cooked and served in small pots with covers known as *pot de crème* pots, although any small baking dishes work well. It is important, however, not to overcook the custard, especially if you plan to serve it cold; the mixture will become too dense during chilling if it has baked too long. Whether served slightly warm or cold, this custard is best eaten on the day it is made. To vary the flavor, use any of the baked custard variations suggested on pages 10 and 11.

To serve in elegant cups that are not ovenproof, try the stirred variation.

Preheat an oven to 300° F.

In a heavy saucepan, combine the cream and vanilla bean. Place over medium-low heat and warm the cream until bubbles form along the edges of the pan; do not let it boil. Remove from the heat and let cool slightly.

In a bowl, break the egg yolks with a fork and lightly beat in the sugar; avoid overbeating at any point to prevent too many air bubbles from forming. Strain the warm cream through a fine-mesh sieve into a pitcher, then gradually stir it into the egg mixture until smooth. Strain the mixture into a pitcher and then carefully pour the custard mixture into 6 to 8 individual heatproof *pot de crème* pots with lids or 6- or 8-ounce custard cups.

Transfer the baking dishes to an ovenproof pan, place the pan in the oven, and pour in enough hot water (not boiling) to reach about two thirds of the way up the sides of the dishes. Cover the pots with their lids or place a sheet of aluminum foil over the ovenproof pan to cover the tops of the custards. Bake until a knife inserted near the edge comes out barely clean, 20 to 30 minutes; the center should still wobble slightly when a container is shaken. Remove the lids or the aluminum foil and transfer the baking dishes to a wire rack.

Serve slightly warm, at room temperature, or cover tightly and chill for several hours.

Makes 6 to 8 servings.

STOVE-TOP VARIATION: In the top of a double boiler, combine the beaten egg yolks with the sugar and whisk until creamy and pale yellow, about 5 minutes. Slowly add the warm cream while whisking until well blended. Place over simmering water and cook, whisking almost constantly, until the mixture forms a custardy texture, 15 to 20 minutes. Strain into a pitcher, then carefully pour into custard cups, cover, and chill overnight.

4 cups heavy (whipping) cream
1 vanilla bean, split lengthwise
10 egg yolks
1 cup sugar

Burnt Cream (*Crème Brûlée*)

4 cups heavy (whipping) cream
10 egg yolks
½ cup granulated sugar, or to taste
About ½ cup firmly packed light brown sugar, sieved and spread out to dry, or superfine granulated sugar

I prefer the French *crème brûlée* to the original English burnt cream. The name comes from the fact that the creamy custard is topped with sugar that is melted and caramelized. This custard actually is just a less sweet variation of a *pot de crème*. Although vanilla is not used in classic *crème brûlée*, you may wish to add a vanilla bean to the simmering cream or stir some pure vanilla extract into the egg-milk mixture. Try the flavor variations suggested on pages 10 and 11.

Tradition dictates that *crème brûlée* be baked in deep custard cups. Today many chefs pour the mixture into shallow ramekins that allow for a larger expanse of the crisp sugar glaze. Restaurants use a heated baker's iron or a salamander to melt the sugar; most home cooks rely on a hot broiler.

Position a rack in the center of an oven and preheat to 300° F.

In a heavy saucepan, place the cream over medium heat and warm the cream until bubbles form along the edges of the pan; do not let it boil. Remove from the heat and let cool slightly.

In a bowl, break the egg yolks with a fork and lightly beat in the sugar; avoid overbeating at any point to prevent too many air bubbles from forming. Strain the cream through a fine-mesh sieve into a pitcher, then gradually stir it into the egg mixture until smooth. Strain the mixture into a pitcher and then carefully pour into six 8-ounce or eight 6-ounce high-heat-resistant custard cups or ramekins.

Transfer the baking dishes to an ovenproof pan, place the pan in the oven, and pour in enough hot water (not boiling) to reach about two thirds of the way up the sides of the baking dishes. Place a sheet of aluminum foil over the pan to cover the tops of the custards loosely. Bake until a knife inserted near the edge of the custard comes out barely clean, 30 to 40 minutes; the center should still wobble slightly when a container is shaken. Regulate oven temperature during baking to maintain water at the almost simmering stage; do not allow to boil. Uncover the pan and remove the baking dishes to a wire rack to cool completely. Cover tightly and refrigerate until well chilled, at least several hours or for as long as overnight.

Position a broiler rack so that the tops of the custards will be about 4 inches from the heat source and preheat the broiler to very hot. Fill a mister bottle with water.

Sprinkle the tops of the custards with a thin, even layer of sugar, making sure that no custard shows through the sugar. Using the mister bottle, lightly moisten the sugar. Arrange all dishes on a baking sheet and place under the broiler until the sugar melts and the tops are bubbly, about 1 minute; watch carefully to avoid scorching. Remove from the oven and let stand for a few minutes to harden the crust. If kept for more than 1 hour, the tops will melt.

Makes 6 to 8 servings.

Stirred Stove-Top Custard

This *is* pudding to many people, whether remembered as ultimate comfort fare or associated with the nursery table. It is what the boxed mixes try to emulate but can not match—a stirred-from-scratch homey rendition.

Although using cornstarch as the thickener yields a smoother pudding, you may choose to substitute about twice as much all-purpose flour. For an even smoother custard, cook the pudding in the top of a double boiler set over simmering water.

My basic recipe for stirred custard is followed by numerous flavor variations. I love vanilla and use both the bean and extract; feel free to omit either one if you prefer a less-pronounced vanilla flavor.

2¾ cups milk
1 cup heavy (whipping) cream, light cream, or half-and-half
1 vanilla bean, split lengthwise
¾ cup sugar, or more to taste
¼ cup cornstarch
Pinch of salt
4 egg yolks, at room temperature
2 tablespoons unsalted butter, softened
2 teaspoons pure vanilla extract

In a heavy saucepan, combine 2 cups of the milk, the cream, and vanilla bean. Place over medium-low heat and warm the mixture until bubbles form around the edges of the pan. Remove the vanilla bean and scrape the seeds into the milk mixture. Keep warm.

In the top pan of a double boiler or in a heavy saucepan, stir together the sugar, cornstarch, and salt. Stir in the remaining ¾ cup milk and mix well. Add the egg yolks and whisk to blend. Strain the warm milk through a fine-mesh sieve into a pitcher, then slowly whisk it into the sugar mixture. Place over simmering water or low heat and cook, stirring or whisking constantly, until thickened, about 10 minutes; do not allow to boil. Cover and cook about 8 minutes longer, whisking or stirring several times. Then, while still over the heat, beat with a hand-held mixer set on medium speed or with a wire whisk until very smooth, about 2 minutes.

Remove from the heat. Add the butter and vanilla extract and stir until the butter melts.

Spoon the custard into 6 individual custard cups or other dessert dishes or into a 2-quart casserole dish. Cover with plastic wrap, pressing it directly onto the surface of the pudding(s). Set aside to serve warm, or cool to room temperature and refrigerate until chilled, at least 2 hours or for as long as 24 hours.

Makes 6 servings.

STIRRED CUSTARD VARIATIONS

STIRRED JUICE PUDDINGS

Not all stirred puddings contain eggs and milk. Try these two refreshing variations.

RED GRITS

German röte grütze and Scandinavian rødgrøt are made from berry juice and thickened with either traditional farina (granular meal made from hard wheat, such as Cream of Wheat) or more modern cornstarch. Fresh raspberries, strawberries, or red currants are most frequently used in "red grits," although any berry or combination of berries works well.

In a saucepan, combine 4 cups berries and 2 cups water. Place over low heat and simmer until the berries render their juice. Press the juice through a fine-mesh sieve into a bowl; discard the pulp. You will need 2 cups juice. Sweeten the berries with about ½ cup sugar, or to taste.

Pour the liquid into a heavy saucepan or into the top pan of a double boiler set over simmering water. Bring the berry juice to a simmer. Slowly sprinkle in ⅓ cup regular Cream of Wheat or other farina, while stirring constantly. Stir in freshly squeezed lemon juice or sweet wine to taste, if desired. Simmer, stirring constantly, until thickened, about 3 minutes over direct heat or about 15 minutes over simmering water.

Follow the preceding recipe for Stirred Stove-Top Custard, making any one of the following changes. Or use the basic recipe to create your own flavored custards.

Almond Custard Pudding. Omit the vanilla bean and substitute almond extract for the vanilla extract. Crumble enough Italian *amaretti* or other almond-flavored macaroons to equal 1 cup fine crumbs. Stir about ⅔ cup of the crumbs into the pudding along with the almond extract. Sprinkle the remaining crumbs over the top of the pudding just before serving.

Butterscotch Custard Pudding. Omit the vanilla bean. Increase the butter to 6 tablespoons and substitute 1¾ cups firmly packed light brown sugar for the granulated sugar. After heating the milk and cream as directed, melt the butter in another heavy saucepan over low heat, add the brown sugar, and stir until the sugar and butter melt together, about 3 minutes. Gradually stir or whisk in the warm cream mixture until smooth. In the top pan of a double boiler, stir together the cornstarch and salt; do not add granulated sugar. Continue as directed in the basic recipe, adding the brown sugar-milk mixture in place of the milk.

Chocolate Custard Pudding. Increase the sugar to 1 cup. Add ¼ to ⅓ cup unsweetened cocoa powder, preferably Dutch-process type, along with the sugar. Increase the butter to ¼ cup (½ stick) or more. Alternatively, omit the cocoa powder and reduce the sugar to ½ cup. Finely chop 6 to 8 ounces semisweet or bittersweet chocolate and stir it into the pudding along with the butter until melted.

Citrus Custard Pudding. Omit the vanilla bean. Add 1 tablespoon finely grated or minced lemon, lime, orange, or tangerine zest to the milk and cream when heating. Strain the milk, if desired, before adding the sugar mixture. Garnish the pudding with candied peel of the same fruit.

Coconut Custard Pudding. Substitute canned or freshly made coconut milk for all or part of the milk and cream. Sprinkle the top of the pudding with lightly toasted sweetened shredded coconut.

Coffee Custard Pudding. Stir about 1 tablespoon instant-espresso powder into the warm milk-cream mixture.

Fresh Fruit Swirl Custard Pudding. Prepare the basic custard and chill. Purée about 2 cups fresh berries or figs, sliced peaches or nectarines, poached pears, cooked apples, or stewed dried fruit until smooth. Swirl it through the cooled pudding.

High Spirited Custard Pudding. For an adult version of this childhood favorite, omit the vanilla bean and stir in Amaretto (almond-flavored liqueur), Frangelico (hazelnut-flavored liqueur), Grand Marnier or other orange-flavored liqueur, Kahlúa or other coffee-flavored liqueur, or other liqueur to taste instead of the vanilla extract.

Mocha Custard Pudding. Prepare the Chocolate Pudding variation above. Stir about 2 teaspoons instant-espresso powder into the warm milk.

Pineapple Custard Pudding. Stir 1 cup canned crushed pineapple into the warm custard.

Alternatively, omit the farina and combine ⅓ cup cornstarch with about ⅓ cup cold water to make a thin paste. While stirring constantly, drizzle the cornstarch mixture into the berry mixture. Then cook, continuing to stir, until the mixture thickens, about 2 minutes over direct heat or about 10 minutes over simmering water.

Remove the custard from the heat and let cool for about 5 minutes. Pour into 4 individual serving containers. Cover and chill until set, about 3 hours. Serve with dollops of Devon cream, *crème fraîche,* or sweetened sour cream.

GRAPE PUDDING

Greek *moustalevria* and Italian *crema fredda di uva nera* are similar custards made from grape juice.

In a heavy saucepan, blend 2 cups cold freshly squeezed or reconstituted thawed frozen grape juice with ¼ cup cornstarch or ½ cup all-purpose flour and stir until smooth. Stir in 2 cups more grape juice. Sweeten with about ½ cup sugar, or to taste. Place over low heat and cook, stirring constantly, until the mixture comes to a simmer. Stirring constantly, simmer until the pudding is thickened, about 5 minutes longer.

Remove from the heat, pour into a bowl, and let cool to room temperature. Distribute 2 cups fresh seedless or seeded grapes among 4 shallow bowls or glasses. Spoon the pudding over the grapes. Cover and refrigerate for at least 3 hours.

Serve with dollops of lightly sweetened whipped cream or vanilla yogurt.

Floating Island

8 egg whites
¼ teaspoon cream of tartar
Pinch of salt
1 cup sugar, preferably superfine
3 cups milk
1 teaspoon pure vanilla extract
Custard Cream (page 88)

This classic meringue dessert, called *oeufs à la neige, île flottante,* or snow eggs, lends itself to infinite variations. For the photograph I prepared the tropical version described on page 24. The egg yolks that remain once you have assembled the egg whites for the meringues can be used for making the custard sauce.

In a mixing bowl, combine the egg whites, cream of tartar, and salt. Using a hand-held mixer, beat until the whites form soft peaks. Beating constantly, gradually add the sugar and continue beating until the egg whites are stiff.

In a large skillet, bring the milk to a slow boil over medium heat. Stir in the vanilla.

Using an ice cream scoop or large spoon rinsed in cold water, scoop up about one sixth of the egg-white mixture and drop it into the slowly boiling milk. Repeat with the remaining egg-white mixture, dipping the scoop or spoon in cold water each time and forming 6 equal scoops in all. Poach the meringues, turning gently with a wooden spoon several times, until set, 2 to 3 minutes; do not overcook. Using a slotted utensil, carefully remove the meringues to a cloth towel to drain well. Strain the poaching milk into a bowl and reserve for making the sauce. Transfer the drained meringues to a platter or tray, cover loosely, and refrigerate until cold, about 2 hours.

Strain the poaching milk into a bowl. Use in the Custard Cream or for another purpose.

Prepare the Custard Cream, using 2 cups of the strained poaching milk or adding more milk if needed. Set aside until serving time. It may be served warm, at room temperature, or chilled.

To serve, ladle some of the sauce onto individual deep plates or shallow bowls and top with a meringue. Alternatively, pour the sauce into a large serving dish and arrange the meringues over the top. Spoon a meringue and a portion of the sauce into individual serving dishes at the table.

Makes 6 servings.

FLOATING ISLAND VARIATIONS

BAKED ISLANDS

Instead of poaching small islands as described in the basic recipe, the meringue mixture may be baked in the manner suggested by Julia Child.

Preheat an oven to 250° F. Butter a 3-quart straight-sided baking dish. Dust with powdered sugar and tap out excess.

Turn the meringue mixture into the prepared dish and bake until the meringue is puffed and a thin wooden skewer inserted in the center comes out clean, about 35 minutes.

Transfer to a wire rack and cool to room temperature; the meringue will sink.

Run a knife blade around the edge of the meringue to loosen it and invert it onto a serving platter. Ladle the custard around it. Cut into chunks at the table. Or, in the kitchen invert the island onto a cutting surface and cut it into 6 pieces. Float on individual dishes as directed in the basic recipe.

Using the preceding recipe for Floating Island as a guide, try these variations.

Caramel Floating Island. Prepare the meringues and the Custard Cream. Have a large bowl of ice water ready. Combine 1 cup sugar and ⅓ cup water in a heavy saucepan and stir well. Place over medium-high heat and bring to a simmer. Remove from the heat and swirl the pan to be sure that the sugar is completely dissolved. Cover the pan, return it to the heat, and heat until boiling rapidly, about 2 minutes. Remove the cover and cook, slowly swirling the pan, until the syrup is a light golden brown (or about 330° F, the light-caramel stage, on a candy thermometer). Remove from the heat and continue swirling the pan for a minute or so. Place the pan in the ice water to halt the cooking and cool the syrup. If necessary, just before serving reheat the caramel until it is syrupy. Ladle some of the custard sauce onto each plate and top with a meringue. Using a fork, drizzle the caramel syrup from the tines over the meringues. Garnish with fresh or crystallized violets, if desired.

Chocolate Floating Island. Prepare the meringue islands and refrigerate. Grate or finely chop 2 ounces milk, semisweet, or bittersweet chocolate and add to the simmering Custard Cream along with 1 tablespoon coffee-flavored liqueur or brandy. Heat until the chocolate melts. Ladle some of the sauce onto each plate and top with a meringue. Sprinkle each island with a little shaved chocolate.

Coffee Floating Island. Prepare the meringue islands and refrigerate. Stir 2 tablespoons plain or flavored instant-coffee powder into the simmering Custard Cream (one of the few good uses that I can think of for those flavored instant-coffee mixes). Ladle some of the sauce onto each plate and top with a meringue. Sprinkle each island with a bit of freshly ground coffee.

Golden Treasure Snow Eggs. Prepare the meringue islands and refrigerate. Add the zest and juice of a mandarin orange or tangerine to the simmering Custard Cream; the zest will be removed when the sauce is strained. Ladle some of the sauce onto each plate and top with a meringue. Sprinkle each island with grated orange or tangerine zest.

Tropical Floating Island. Prepare the meringue islands and refrigerate. Replace the milk and cream in the Custard Cream with canned or freshly made coconut milk. In a food processor or blender, pureé the pulp of 2 medium-sized mangoes with sugar and freshly squeezed lime juice to taste; cover and refrigerate until serving time. Purée 2 cups raspberries or hulled strawberries with ¼ cup fresh passion fruit juice or passion fruit liqueur and sugar and lemon juice to taste; cover and refrigerate until serving time. Ladle some of the Custard Cream onto each plate. Spoon small pools of the mango sauce and passion fruit sauce onto the custard, then draw a wooden skewer through the sauces to create a pattern. Add the meringue islands and sprinkle each with lightly toasted sweetened shredded coconut.

Spanish Floating Island *(Natillas)*

Throughout Mexico and the Southwest, the custard and egg whites that go into a floating island are stirred together. I've added lime and cinnamon to the custard to make it reminiscent of Mexican rice pudding. The dish is even more delicious when served with ripe mango slices or cubes.

In a saucepan, combine 3 cups of the milk, lime zest, cinnamon stick, and vanilla bean (if used). Place over medium heat and bring almost to a boil. Remove from the heat and let steep for about 30 minutes. Strain through a fine-mesh sieve into a pitcher. Scrape the seeds from the vanilla bean into the milk mixture.

In a heavy saucepan or the top pan of a double boiler, stir together the cornstarch, sugar, and salt. Whisk or beat in the egg yolks. Stir in the remaining 1 cup milk to make a thick paste. Slowly add the warm milk, whisking or stirring constantly, until the mixture is smooth. Place over medium-low heat or over simmering water. Cook, stirring constantly, until thickened, about 30 minutes; do not allow to boil. Remove from the heat and stir in the vanilla extract (if used). Cool to room temperature.

In a mixing bowl, beat the egg whites until foamy. Add the cream of tartar and continue beating until they are stiff but not dry. Gently fold the whites into the custard; do not totally blend together. Pour into a large serving bowl or 6 to 8 individual bowls. Serve immediately or cover and chill for up to 4 hours. Just before serving, grate nutmeg to taste over the top or pass a nutmeg grater at the table.

Makes 6 servings.

4 cups milk
Zest of 1 lime, removed in 1 or 2 long
     strips
One 3-inch cinnamon stick
1 vanilla bean, split lengthwise, or
     1 teaspoon pure vanilla extract
¼ cup cornstarch
¾ cup sugar
Pinch of salt
5 eggs, separated
½ teaspoon cream of tartar
Nutmeg for grating

Whipped Wine Custard
(*Zabaglione* or *Sabayon*)

6 egg yolks
⅓ cup sugar, or to taste
Pinch of salt
½ cup Marsala wine or other wine or
    spirit (see recipe introduction)

Italians make their frothy zabaglione with Marsala wine. French cooks are more likely to prepare sabayon with dry sherry, Madeira, or vermouth or with sparkling or dessert wines. For a different flavor, combine the wine with a spirit such as bourbon, rum, or Calvados or other brandy, or add a favorite liqueur such as praline or Frangelico (hazelnut flavored). Citrus juice and zest, vanilla, or ground ginger or other spices may be added along with the wine.

Although the custard may be eaten on its own, it is frequently served with fresh berries, sliced peaches or nectarines, poached pears, or candied fruits. Or offer *biscotti* or other cookies for dipping into the custard.

In a round-bottomed copper zabaglione pan or the top pan of a double boiler, combine the egg yolks, sugar, and salt. Using a wire whisk or hand-held mixer, beat until the eggs are pale and creamy, about 3 minutes. Slowly whisk in the wine.

Place over gently simmering (not boiling) water. Continue to beat constantly until the custard is thick and doubled in volume, 5 to 8 minutes; it should just hold its shape. Spoon into stemmed glasses or pour into custard cups and serve warm.

Makes 4 servings.

VARIATIONS: For a lighter custard, beat 6 egg whites until stiff peaks form. Fold them into the warm custard just before serving.

For a cold dessert that holds its shape, remove the warm custard from the heat and place the pan in a bowl of ice cubes to cool rapidly. Beat 2 cups heavy (whipping) cream until it holds its shape. Using a rubber spatula, fold the whipped cream into the custard. Cover and chill or freeze. Remove from the freezer a few minutes before serving.

Mocha Tapioca

For those who have bad associations with tapioca from school cafeterias, this grown-up version of custard thickened with tapioca instead of cornstarch or flour may change a few minds.

If you use quick-cooking tapioca, eliminate the soaking step. The pearl type results in a creamier pudding and I like the little "fish eyes," which are actually beads formulated from the starch found in the roots of the tropical manioc plant *(Manihot esculenta)*.

In a bowl, combine the pearl tapioca and water. Cover and let stand until most of the water is absorbed, about 3 hours for small-pearl type or overnight for large-pearl tapioca. Drain well.

In the top pan of a double boiler, combine the cocoa and sugar and stir well. Stir in the espresso and enough of the milk to make a thin paste. Add the drained pearl tapioca or the quick-cooking tapioca, the remaining milk, and the lemon zest. Place over simmering water and cook, stirring occasionally, until the tapioca turns translucent and is tender when tasted, about 10 minutes for quick-cooking tapioca or about 30 minutes for small-pearl tapioca or about 1½ hours for large-pearl type. Remove from the heat.

In a bowl, beat the egg yolks until light colored. Stir about ½ cup of the hot pudding into the yolks, then stir the mixture into the pudding. Discard the lemon zest. Stir in the liqueur, brandy, or vanilla. Spoon into 4 serving dishes.

Serve warm or at room temperature, or cover and refrigerate for several hours or as long as overnight. In any case, top with dollops of Whipped Cream.

Makes 4 servings.

¾ cup pearl tapioca, or 6 tablespoons quick-cooking tapioca
1½ cups water
¼ cup unsweetened cocoa powder, preferably Dutch-process type
¾ cup sugar, or more to taste
2 tablespoons instant espresso powder dissolved in ¼ cup hot water, then cooled
1½ cups milk
Zest of 1 lemon, removed with a vegetable peeler in 1 or 2 long strips
2 egg yolks
About 1 tablespoon Amaretto or other liqueur or brandy, or to taste, or 1 teaspoon pure vanilla extract
Whipped Cream (page 91)

English Trifle

Stirred Stove-Top Custard (page 19)
6 cups fresh blueberries, raspberries, or strawberries, coarsely chopped
Sugar
2 cups Lemon Curd (page 92 or purchase a good-tasting version in a jar)
A sponge cake layer about 11 by 18 inches or a pound cake (use a favorite recipe or purchase a high-quality product)
About ½ cup dry sherry
Whipped Cream (page 91) for topping
Fresh berries (same as used in trifle) for garnish
Whole fresh mint leaves or sprigs for garnish

To show off the multicolored layers of a trifle, choose a clear glass bowl or individual containers. Use my basic recipe as a guide to layer any cake, jam or fruit sauce, fresh fruit, and custard.

Prepare the custard and let cool to room temperature.

In a bowl, lightly sweeten the berries with sugar to taste.

To assemble, spoon a thin layer of the Lemon Curd in the bottom of a 2½-quart bowl or 6 to 8 individual containers. Top with a layer of custard ¼ to ½ inch thick. Slice the cake ¼ to ½ inch thick. Cut the slices to fit inside the serving dish and line the dish. If necessary, trim several pieces to form a single layer; use trimmings to fill any holes in the cake layer. Sprinkle the cake layer with sherry to moisten. Spoon on enough Lemon Curd to cover the cake with a thin layer, spoon on a layer of the chopped berries, top the fruit with another layer of the custard, and then another cake layer. Continue to layer in this manner until all the ingredients are used, ending with the custard.

Cover and refrigerate for at least 6 hours or overnight.

Just before serving, cover the top of the trifle with Whipped Cream, crown it with a few dollops of the Lemon Curd, and swirl to create a pattern. Garnish with fresh berries and mint leaves.

If prepared in a large container, spoon up the dessert at the table.

Makes 8 servings.

Piña Colada Trifle

Perhaps this trifle got a bit too tipsy and ended up tossed together instead of in traditional neat layers. Offer Whipped Cream (page 91) or crème fraîche when serving.

I make this for parties, but the recipe can be cut in half for smaller groups.

In the top pan of a double boiler, combine 1 cup of the milk, egg yolks, and cornstarch and whisk to form a thick paste. Whisk in the remaining 1 cup milk and the condensed milk. Set over simmering (not boiling) water and cook, whisking or stirring constantly, until thickened to the consistency of a creamy sauce, about 20 minutes; it should coat the back of a spoon, and your finger should leave a trail when you trace it across the spoon. Remove the custard from the heat and stir in the vanilla. Set aside to cool.

Cut the cake into 1-inch cubes and place them in a 2½-quart serving dish. Drain the crushed and sliced pineapple and set aside, reserving ½ cup of the pineapple juice. Sprinkle the cake with the pineapple juice and rum. Add the crushed pineapple and about two thirds of the coconut and toss lightly with the cake. Pour about half of the custard over the cake and stir to mix well. Cover with the remaining custard. Cover the container and refrigerate for about 4 hours.

Just before serving, cut the pineapple rings in half and arrange them over the top of the custard. Sprinkle with the remaining coconut.

Makes 8 servings.

2½ cups milk or fresh or canned coconut milk
2 cans (14 ounces *each*) sweetened condensed milk
4 egg yolks, beaten
½ cup cornstarch
1 teaspoon pure vanilla extract
A sponge cake layer about 11 by 18 inches or a pound cake (use a favorite recipe or purchase a high-quality product)
1 can (20 ounces) crushed pineapple, or 2 cups chopped fresh pineapple
1 can (8 ounces) sliced pineapple, or about 6 slices cored fresh pineapple (about ¼ inch thick)
½ cup light rum
1½ cups freshly grated or sweetened dried coconut

Mawmaw Mackie's Banana Pudding

3 eggs, separated (use whites toward
    making the Meringue Topping)
1 cup sugar
1½ tablespoons cornstarch
Pinch of salt
3 cups milk or half-and-half
¼ cup (½ stick) softened unsalted
    butter
1½ teaspoons pure vanilla extract
About 30 vanilla wafers
6 ripe bananas
Meringue Topping (page 91)

My grandmother Izetta McNair made the best version of this American classic that I've ever tasted. Unfortunately no one in my family wrote down just how she made her divine creation, which she always did without looking at a recipe, of course. My aunt Pauline Wiggington and I have each come close to duplicating Mawmaw Mackie's pudding, but nothing quite lives up to the taste stored in my memory. Perhaps it was the farm-fresh ingredients. Or perhaps it wasn't really any better, but rather just idealized in my childhood memories.

In a heavy saucepan, combine the egg yolks, sugar, cornstarch, and salt. Whisk or stir in the milk or half-and-half, a little at a time, until the mixture is smooth. Place over medium heat and cook, stirring and scraping the bottom constantly, until the mixture thickens, 8 to 10 minutes. Reduce the heat to very low and cook, stirring constantly, for about 3 minutes longer. Remove from the heat, add the butter and vanilla, and stir until the butter melts.

Line a 2-quart baking dish or casserole with half of the vanilla wafers. Peel the bananas and slice crosswise about ¼ inch thick. Arrange half of the banana slices over the wafers. Cover with about half of the warm custard. Top with the remaining vanilla wafers in a single layer, then the remaining banana slices. Cover with the remaining custard. Let stand until cool.

Preheat an oven to 350° F.

Prepare the meringue. Spread the meringue over the custard, making sure that the meringue touches the inner edge of the baking dish to prevent weeping and shrinkage. Using a spatula or knife blade, swirl the top of the egg whites decoratively. Bake until lightly browned, about 10 minutes.

To prevent shrinkage of the baked meringue, transfer the pudding to a draft-free place that is not too cold and let stand until serving. Serve at room temperature.

Makes 6 servings.

VARIATIONS: Omit the banana slices. Use 4 cups well-drained, crushed canned pineapple, chopped fresh pineapple, or sliced ripe papayas or mangoes.

Bavarian Cream

Also known in France as a *bavarois,* this custard-based dessert is lightened with whipped cream and stabilized with gelatin; for a creamier texture, reduce the amount of gelatin by half. Bavarians are generally set in a mold and well chilled, then turned out for serving.

Prepare the Custard Cream. Have a large bowl of ice water ready.

Meanwhile, in a small saucepan, combine the gelatin and water and stir until blended. Set aside to soften for about 5 minutes. Place over medium heat and stir until the gelatin dissolves, about 2 minutes. Strain the warm Custard Cream into a bowl and stir in the dissolved gelatin to mix well. Set the bowl in the ice water. Refrigerate, stirring frequently, until the mixture takes on a syrupy consistency and just begins to set.

Meanwhile, in a chilled bowl, beat the cream until it begins to hold its shape. Add the powdered sugar and beat until it forms soft peaks; do not overbeat. Cover and refrigerate until the custard mixture begins to set, then fold the cream into the custard.

Lightly brush the inside of a 1½-quart metal ring or other mold or six 1-cup molds with vegetable oil or melted butter. Turn the cream mixture into the mold(s), smooth the top(s), cover tightly, and refrigerate until firmly set, about 8 hours.

To unmold, dip the bottoms of the mold(s) briefly into hot water, run a knife blade around the edges to loosen them, then cover with a serving plate(s) and invert. Lift off the mold(s). Garnish with berries or fruit and mint.

Makes 6 servings.

VARIATIONS: Add any one of the following to the milk when making the Custard Cream, varying amounts to taste: 1 tablespoon instant-espresso powder; 4 ounces high-quality sweetened chocolate, melted; grated zest of 2 lemons, limes, oranges, or tangerines; or 1 tablespoon liqueur of choice. Or fold 1½ cups puréed fresh berries or soft-fruit pulp into the custard before chilling.

Custard Cream (page 88)
½ cup cold water
2 envelopes (2 scant tablespoons) unflavored gelatin
1½ cups heavy (whipping) cream, well chilled
¼ cup powdered sugar
Vegetable oil or melted unsalted butter for brushing molds
Fresh berries or sliced fruit for garnish
Fresh mint leaves or sprigs for garnish

Spiced Maple-Pumpkin Charlotte

Use this basic technique for forming charlotte linings from any bakery product, then fill with any mousse or Bavarian cream.

To make the Moistening Syrup, in a small, heavy saucepan, combine the sugar and cool water. Place over high heat and heat, stirring constantly, until the sugar completely dissolves. Pour into a shallow bowl to cool, then stir in the 3 tablespoons brandy or rum (if used).

Prepare the Custard Cream. Strain through a fine-mesh sieve into a large bowl.

In a heatproof cup, stir the hot water and gelatin together, then place in a pan of simmering water and heat, stirring constantly, until the gelatin dissolves. Add it to the Custard Cream and stir until the mixture cools to room temperature.

To make the Maple-Pumpkin Flavoring, in a bowl, combine the puréed pumpkin or squash, syrup, cinnamon, ginger, nutmeg, allspice, salt, and vanilla, brandy, or rum. Add the Custard Cream and mix well.

Cut a parchment- or waxed-paper circle to fit the bottom of a 2-quart charlotte mold or soufflé dish, or eight 1-cup individual molds. Place the paper in the bottom and lightly butter the sides of the mold(s). Or butter the bottom and sides of an 8-inch springform pan. Lightly brush the ladyfingers with the Moistening Syrup and tightly line the sides of the charlotte mold(s) or soufflé dish with the ladyfingers; if necessary, cut ladyfingers so they are even with the top rim of the mold. Or line the bottom and sides of the springform pan.

In a chilled bowl, beat the cream until it begins to hold its shape. Add the powdered sugar and whip until it forms soft peaks; do not overbeat. Stir about ½ cup of the whipped cream into the custard mixture to lighten it, then fold in the remaining whipped cream, incorporating well. Turn the custard mixture into the lined mold(s). If using a charlotte mold(s) or soufflé dish, cover the top with ladyfingers. Cover tightly and chill until firmly set, about 6 hours or as long as overnight.

Prepare the Praline Topping (if used). Set aside.

To serve, briefly dip the bottom of the charlotte mold(s) or soufflé dish into a pan of hot water. Run a knife blade around the edges to loosen them, then cover with a serving plate(s) and invert. If using a springform pan, remove the clamp-on ring and transfer the charlotte to a serving plate. Pipe rosettes of whipped cream around the edge of the charlotte(s) and sprinkle the center(s) with the Praline Topping (if used).

Makes 8 servings.

MOISTENING SYRUP

⅓ cup sugar
⅓ cup cool water
About 3 tablespoons brandy or rum (optional)

Custard Cream (page 88)
¼ cup hot water
1½ envelopes (1½ scant tablespoons) unflavored gelatin

MAPLE-PUMPKIN FLAVORING

2 cups puréed cooked pumpkin or other winter squash, or 1 can (1 pound) pumpkin purée (not pumpkin pie filling)
½ cup maple syrup, or to taste
1 teaspoon ground cinnamon
1 teaspoon ground ginger
¼ teaspoon freshly grated nutmeg
⅛ teaspoon ground allspice
½ teaspoon salt
2 teaspoons pure vanilla extract, brandy, or rum

Softened unsalted butter for greasing mold
About 30 ladyfingers (use a favorite recipe or purchase)
1½ cups heavy (whipping) cream, well chilled
¼ cup powdered sugar
Whipped Cream (page 91) in a pastry bag fitted with rosette tip for piping
Praline Topping (page 93; optional)

CHARLOTTE VARIATIONS

MOLDS AND LINERS

French charlotte molds are made of metal with slightly flared sides that allow the set charlotte to slip out easily when inverted. In lieu of such molds, or for a change of shape or size, charlottes can be molded in springform pans, gelatin molds, straight-sided soufflé dishes, bowls, loaf pans, and cake pans. When forming charlottes in a container without the traditional flared sides, the bottom and sides of the container may be lined with parchment paper, waxed paper, or dampened cheesecloth before adding the bakery product; this makes unmolding easier.

For individual-sized charlottes, choose custard cups, bowls, or small molds such as timbales.

In addition to the usual delicate ladyfingers or sponge cake slices, chilled charlottes can be encased in madeleines (scallop-shaped soft cookies); pound cake, bread, or jelly-roll slices; cookies; or other bakery products.

Omit the Maple-Pumpkin Flavoring Mixture in the preceding charlotte recipe. Follow the directions for assembling the charlotte, using one of the suggested variations.

Banana Charlotte. Line the mold with pound cake slices brushed with Moistening Syrup flavored with banana liqueur. Prepare Custard Cream and combine with the dissolved warm gelatin. Fold the whipped cream into the cooled custard. Beginning and ending with the custard mixture, alternate layers with sliced ripe banana (about 5 bananas). After unmolding, decorate with Whipped Cream (page 91) and more banana slices.

Berry Charlotte. Line the mold with sponge cake slices brushed with raspberry-flavored liqueur or berry juice instead of the Moistening Syrup. Prepare the Custard Cream and combine with the dissolved warm gelatin. Fold the whipped cream mixture into the cooled custard. Purée 3 to 4 cups fresh berries, strain through a sieve to remove seeds, sweeten to taste, and fold them into the custard. After unmolding, decorate with whipped crème fraîche and fresh berries. Serve with Fresh Berry Sauce (page 90).

Butterscotch Charlotte. Line the mold with ladyfingers brushed with Moistening Syrup flavored with scotch. Substitute Butterscotch Pudding (page 20) for the Custard Cream and combine with the dissolved warm gelatin. Fold the whipped cream into the cooled custard. After unmolding, decorate with Whipped Cream (page 91) flavored with scotch and garnish with crystallized or pesticide-free fresh violets.

Chestnut Charlotte. Line the mold with ladyfingers or other bakery product brushed with Moistening Syrup flavored with Frangelico (hazelnut-flavored liqueur). Prepare the Bavarian Cream filling (page 39). Whip 1 can (15½ ounces) unsweetened chestnut purée until smooth and fold it into the cooled cream filling along with the whipped cream. Stir in about 3 tablespoons chopped glazed chestnuts *(marrons glacés)*. After unmolding, garnish with dollops of Whipped Cream (page 91) flavored with brandy and whole glazed chestnuts.

Chocolate-Raspberry Charlotte. Line the mold with pound cake slices brushed with raspberry-flavored liqueur. Fill with Chocolate Mousse (page 49). After unmolding, decorate with Whipped Cream (page 91), garnish with chocolate curls and raspberries, and serve with Custard Cream (page 88).

Coffee Charlotte. Line the mold with pound cake slices or ladyfingers brushed with espresso or coffee-flavored liqueur. Fill with the Bavarian Cream filling, coffee variation (page 39). After unmolding, decorate with Whipped Cream (page 91), garnish with chocolate-covered coffee beans, and serve with warm Chocolate Sauce (page 89) on the side.

Hazelnut Charlotte. Line the mold with ladyfingers or other bakery products brushed with Frangelico (hazelnut-flavored liqueur). Fill with the Bavarian Cream filling (page 39), flavored with Frangelico to taste. After unmolding, drizzle with warm Chocolate Sauce (page 89) and sprinkle with Glazed Spiced Nuts (page 93), made with hazelnuts.

White Chocolate Charlotte. Line the mold with sponge cake slices brushed with raspberry-flavored liqueur or simple syrup. Fill with White Chocolate Mousse (page 50). After unmolding, drizzle with Chocolate Glaze (page 91). Serve with Whipped Cream (page 91) and Fresh Berry Sauce (page 90).

BAKED APPLE CHARLOTTE

Remove the crusts from about 12 thin slices of white bread or sponge cake and trim pieces to fit the bottom, sides, and top of the mold (see basic recipe for mold sizes). Dip one side of the bread or cake slices in melted butter and use them to line the bottom and sides of the mold, buttered side out and overlapping slices slightly. Reserve the leftover slices for using on top.

Preheat an oven to 400° F.

Peel, core, and thinly slice 3 to 4 pounds tart apples. Heat ¼ cup (½ stick) unsalted butter in a sauté pan or skillet over medium-high heat. Add the apple slices and sauté until the apples render some juice. Stir in 1 cup sugar, or to taste, 3 tablespoons freshly squeezed lemon juice, and 2 teaspoons minced or grated lemon zest. Reduce the heat to medium-low and cook until the apples are reduced to a thick purée, about 35 minutes. Stir in ½ cup apricot preserves. Spoon into the lined mold and pack tightly. Trim bread or cake slices so that they are level with the apples. Cover the apple mixture completely with the reserved bread or cake slices.

Bake in the preheated oven until the bread or cake is golden, about 40 minutes; about midway during cooking, press the top of the charlotte down with a metal spatula to compact the filling. Remove to a wire rack and let cool for about 15 minutes.

Serve warm with Warm Liquor Sauce (page 90), made with Calvados.

Tiramisù

5 egg yolks
½ cup powdered sugar
Pinch of salt
1 pound mascarpone cheese
About 2 cups cold espresso or other
    strong, dark-brewed coffee
About 30 ladyfingers
6 ounces milk or semisweet chocolate,
    grated or shaved with a vegetable
    peeler

Although I prefer the ladyfingers that are commonly used in Italy, this "pick me up" will be more delicate if made with slices of sponge cake. Mascarpone, a rich Italian cream cheese, may be found in cheese stores and specialty-food markets. For a fluffier version, beat 4 egg whites until stiff peaks form and fold them into the mascarpone mixture.

If desired, add hazelnut-, coffee-, or orange-flavored liqueur or dry Marsala to taste to the coffee before dipping the ladyfingers.

In a mixing bowl, combine the egg yolks, sugar, and salt. Whisk or beat using a hand-held mixer until thick and pale yellow, about 5 minutes. Add the mascarpone and beat until the mixture is smooth and thick. Set aside.

Pour the coffee into a shallow bowl. Dip some of the ladyfingers in the coffee and use them to line the bottom and sides of 6 large coffee cups or a 2½-quart straight-sided bowl. Spoon in about half of the mascarpone mixture and sprinkle with about half of the chocolate. Dip the remaining ladyfingers in the coffee and arrange them in a single layer atop the mascarpone. Top with the remaining mascarpone mixture and sprinkle the remaining chocolate over the top.

Cover and refrigerate for at least 4 hours or overnight. If made in a single bowl, spoon into individual dishes when serving.

Makes 6 servings.

MOUSSES

A mousse is a blend of whipped ingredients that are folded together to form a light, fluffy cold dessert. Classic French mousses are made without gelatin, although many cooks today add a bit to ensure that the mousse holds its shape. A "cold soufflé" is a mousse that contains gelatin. It is poured into a mold with a paper ring collar that helps the mousse mixture to stand above the rim of the mold, then it is chilled or frozen until firmly set.

It has been suggested that the light and fluffy British dessert known as a fool (or sometimes foule) takes its name from the fact that it is so easy to make that even a fool can do it. The word for this dessert actually comes from the French *fouler,* "to crush," since fresh fruit is crushed or puréed, then sweetened and chilled before it is folded into whipped cream.

STORING

Mousses must be well chilled before serving, normally several hours or overnight. During such lengthy refrigeration, these delicate beauties can easily take on odors and flavors from foods that are stored nearby. Before chilling, be certain that the dessert and all the foods that will share refrigerator space are tightly covered.

Do not keep any of these ephemeral desserts for more than 24 hours.

Chocolate Mousse

Here are two versions of this beloved dessert. Since classic mousse uses uncooked egg yolks, some people may prefer the very simple yet rich-tasting eggless version.

For a whimsical presentation, prepare both Chocolate Mousse and White Chocolate Mousse (page 48) and layer them in tall glasses, similar to a parfait, or swirl them together in a bowl to create a marbleized effect.

To make the classic mousse, in the top pan of a double boiler set over simmering (not boiling) water, place the chocolate and butter. Stir constantly until they melt. Alternatively, melt in a microwave at half power, stirring several times. Remove from the heat and whisk in the 5 egg yolks, one at a time, until smooth. Transfer to a bowl and stir in the vanilla. Cover and refrigerate.

In a chilled bowl, beat the cream until it forms soft peaks; do not overbeat. Cover and refrigerate.

In the bowl of an electric mixer, combine the egg whites and cream of tartar. Beat until the whites form soft peaks. Continuing to beat, gradually sprinkle in the sugar and beat until the whites form stiff, shiny peaks but are not dry. Stir about one fourth of the whites into the chocolate mixture to lighten it, then fold in the remaining whites and the whipped cream, incorporating well.

To make the eggless mousse, have a large bowl of ice ready. In a saucepan, combine the chocolate and cream. Place over medium-low heat until the chocolate begins to melt and the cream is almost simmering. Whisk or stir until the chocolate and cream are smooth. Stir in the vanilla and sugar to taste. Remove from the heat and place in the bowl of ice. Whisk until creamy smooth and softly holds its shape.

For either version, spoon the mousse into 6 individual bowls or glasses or a 1½-quart serving bowl. Cover tightly and chill for about 2 hours. Serve with dollops of softly whipped cream (if used).

Each version makes 6 servings.

COFFEE VARIATIONS: For Mocha Mousse, follow the classic mousse recipe. Add about 1 tablespoon instant-espresso powder dissolved in 1 tablespoon hot water to the warm chocolate mixture.

For Coffee Mousse, omit the chocolate in the classic mousse. Add about 2 tablespoons instant-espresso powder dissolved in 2 tablespoons water, or to taste, to the melted butter before adding the egg yolks.

CLASSIC CHOCOLATE MOUSSE

8 ounces high-quality semisweet or bittersweet chocolate (not chips), finely chopped
6 tablespoons (¾ stick) unsalted butter, softened
3 eggs, separated
2 egg yolks
2 teaspoons pure vanilla extract
1 cup heavy (whipping) cream, well chilled
Pinch of cream of tartar
3 tablespoons sugar, preferably superfine

EGGLESS CHOCOLATE MOUSSE

8 ounces high-quality semisweet or bittersweet chocolate, finely chopped
2 cups heavy (whipping) cream, well chilled
2 teaspoons pure vanilla extract
About ½ cup powdered sugar

Whipped Cream (page 91) for topping (optional)

White Chocolate Mousse

2 cups heavy (whipping) cream, well chilled
2 cups sugar
½ cup water
½ cup egg whites (3 or 4 eggs)
Pinch of cream of tartar
1 pound high-quality white chocolate, finely chopped

Back in the days when I had the Twin Peaks Grocery in San Francisco, our kitchen turned out vats of this scrumptious froth to satisfy the demands of numerous customers who couldn't seem to get their fill. Be sure to use white chocolate that contains cocoa butter, not the white coating chocolate made with vegetable oils.

I like to serve this mousse in Chocolate Containers (page 92) or Crisp Cookie Cups (page 92) set on a pool of Fresh Berry Sauce (page 90) made from a blend of strawberries and raspberries.

In a chilled bowl, whip the cream until it forms soft peaks; do not overbeat. Cover and refrigerate.

In a saucepan, combine the sugar and water. Place over high heat and cook, without stirring, until the mixture registers 250° F on a candy thermometer or forms a hard but pliable ball when a few drops are added to cold water. Remove from the heat.

Meanwhile, in the bowl of an electric mixer, combine the egg whites and cream of tartar. Beat until the whites form soft peaks. Continuing to beat, drizzle the hot sugar syrup into the egg whites. After adding all of the syrup, beat the mixture for about 3 minutes at high speed. Add the white chocolate and beat until the chocolate melts and is well blended into the egg-white mixture, about 1 minute. Transfer to a bowl and let cool to room temperature.

Fold the chilled whipped cream into the egg-white mixture, incorporating well. Cover and chill until set, about 3 hours or overnight.

Makes 8 servings.

Citrus Orchard Mousse

Any citrus juice and zest or a combination of different citrus may be used in this airy dessert.

In the top pan of a double boiler, using a wire whisk or a hand-held mixer, beat the 5 egg yolks until very thick and pale yellow, about 5 minutes. Gradually beat in 1 cup sugar if using lime or lemon juice, or ½ cup sugar if using orange or tangerine juice; adjust amount of sugar to taste and tartness of the fruit. Stir in the citrus juice and zest (if used). Place over simmering water and cook, whisking or beating continuously, until thick enough to coat the back of a metal spoon, about 5 minutes; do not overcook or the mixture will curdle. Pour into a bowl and let cool to room temperature.

In a chilled bowl, whip the cream until it forms soft peaks; do not overbeat. Cover and refrigerate.

In the bowl of an electric mixer, combine the egg whites, cream of tartar, and salt. Beat the egg whites until stiff and shiny but not dry. Stir about one fourth of the beaten egg whites into the citrus mixture to lighten it. Fold in the remaining egg whites and all of the whipped cream, incorporating well. Turn into 6 to 8 individual serving dishes or glasses or a serving bowl, cover tightly, and chill until the mousse is set, about 3 hours or as long as overnight.

Garnish each serving with citrus slices and mint.

Makes 6 to 8 servings.

3 eggs, separated
2 egg yolks
½ to 1 cup sugar
¾ cup freshly squeezed citrus juice
1 tablespoon freshly grated citrus zest (optional)
1 cup heavy (whipping) cream, well chilled
Pinch of cream of tartar
Pinch of salt
Thinly sliced citrus slices for garnish
Fresh mint sprigs for garnish

Margarita Mousse

½ cup cold water
1 envelope (scant 1 tablespoon)
    unflavored gelatin
6 eggs, separated
1 cup sugar
¾ cup freshly squeezed lime juice
½ cup tequila
⅓ cup Triple Sec
1 cup heavy (whipping) cream, well
    chilled
Pinch of cream of tartar
Pinch of salt
Lime wedges for moistening glass
    rims
Sugar for frosting glass rims
Lime wedges for garnish

A perfect dessert for a hot summer day. Serve in wide goblets with rims frosted with sugar to recall a salty margarita. Due to the alcohol, this mousse does not store well; plan to consume it the day it is made.

In a small bowl, combine ¼ cup of the water and the gelatin and stir well. Set aside to soften for about 5 minutes.

In a large bowl, using a wire whisk or hand-held mixer, beat the egg yolks until they are very thick and pale yellow, about 5 minutes. Set aside.

In a saucepan, combine ½ cup of the sugar with the remaining ¼ cup water and ¼ cup of the lime juice. Place over high heat and bring to a boil. Cook, without stirring, until the sugar dissolves, 2 to 3 minutes. Remove from the heat and stir in the softened gelatin until the gelatin dissolves. Stir in the tequila, Triple Sec, and the remaining ½ cup lime juice.

Slowly drizzle the hot sugar-liquid mixture into the beaten egg yolks, whisking vigorously until smooth. Place the bowl in a larger bowl filled with ice until it just begins to thicken, using a rubber spatula to scrape the bottom and sides of the bowl frequently; do not let the mixture set completely.

In a chilled bowl, beat the cream until it forms soft peaks; do not overbeat. Cover and refrigerate.

In the bowl of an electric mixer, combine the egg whites, cream of tartar, and salt. Beat until the whites form soft peaks. Continuing to beat, gradually sprinkle in the remaining ½ cup sugar and beat until the whites form stiff, shiny peaks but are not dry. Set aside.

When the egg yolk mixture begins to thicken to a syrupy consistency, stir about one fourth of the beaten egg whites into it to lighten it. Fold in the remaining egg whites and all of the whipped cream, incorporating well. Cover tightly and refrigerate for about 4 hours.

Just before serving, moisten the rims of 8 stemmed glasses with lime juice. Pour a layer of sugar in a saucer and, one at a time, dip the moistened glass rims into the sugar to adhere it to the rim. Spoon the mousse into the glasses and garnish each serving with a lime wedge.

Makes 8 servings.

Fruit Mousse

Use this recipe as a guide with a wide variety of perfectly ripe berries or fruit. Soft ripe fruits such as figs, guavas, or peaches only need to be peeled and pitted before the pulp is puréed. Firm fruits such as apples or dried fruits must be cooked until soft before puréeing. Omit the gelatin if you want a very light and creamy mousse that will be served within a few hours and spoon the mixture into stemmed glasses before chilling.

Select a 1-quart soufflé dish or six 5-ounce ceramic or glass dishes with straight sides. Cut strips of waxed paper that are long enough to encircle the container(s). Wrap a double layer of the paper around the dish(es) so that it forms a straight collar that extends about 2 inches above the top of the container(s). Secure with tape, string, or rubber bands. Set aside.

Place the fruit in a food processor or blender and purée; if using berries, pass them through a sieve set over a bowl to remove the seeds. Transfer to a saucepan and sweeten the puree to taste with about ½ cup granulated sugar (make it a bit sweeter than usual to compensate for the chilling). Stir in the gelatin (if used). Place over low heat and stir until the sugar and gelatin dissolve. Stir in the lemon juice or liqueur to taste; set aside to cool.

In a chilled bowl, beat the cream with the powdered sugar until it forms soft peaks; do not overbeat. Cover and refrigerate.

In the bowl of an electric mixer, combine the egg whites, cream of tartar, and salt. Beat until the whites form soft peaks. Continuing to beat, slowly sprinkle in the 2 tablespoons granulated sugar and beat until the whites form stiff, shiny peaks but are not dry. Stir about one fourth of the beaten egg whites into the purée to lighten it, then fold in the remaining egg whites and the whipped cream, incorporating well. Spoon into the prepared dish(es). Place in the freezer until well set, about 3 hours or overnight; cover the top(s) as soon as the mousse is set.

To serve, peel off the waxed paper collar(s) from the dish(es). Garnish with fresh fruit and flowers (if used).

Makes 6 servings.

4 cups fresh berries, or 2 cups peeled and sliced fresh fruit (see recipe introduction)

About ½ cup plus 2 tablespoons granulated sugar

1 envelope (scant 1 tablespoon) unflavored gelatin (if making a cold soufflé or holding for more than 2 hours)

About 2 tablespoons freshly squeezed lemon juice or fruit-flavored liqueur (choose a flavor compatible with the fruit, such as framboise with raspberries, Amaretto with peaches, or Grand Marnier with apricots)

1 cup heavy (whipping) cream, well chilled

¼ cup sifted powdered sugar

4 egg whites

¼ teaspoon cream of tartar

Pinch of salt

Fresh fruit (same as used in mousse) for garnish

Pesticide-free non-toxic flowers such as lavender or strawberry blossoms (optional)

Roseberry Fool

For this old-fashioned English treat, a first cousin to mousse, choose the season's most flavorful berries, such as raspberries, blackberries, blueberries, or strawberries. If the taste of rose water or syrup is too perfumed for you, flavor the cream with berry- or orange-flavored liqueur or pure vanilla extract.

In a food processor or in a bowl with a fork, coarsely purée or crush the berries. If desired, pass the fruit through a wire sieve to remove seeds. Lightly sweeten to taste with granulated sugar. Cover and refrigerate until well chilled.

In a chilled bowl, whip the cream until it begins to thicken. Add the powdered sugar and the rose water or syrup to taste. Continue beating until the cream holds its shape. Using a rubber spatula, gently fold the chilled berries and their juice into the whipped cream.

Spoon the berry mixture into 6 clear bowls, stemmed glasses, or parfait glasses. Garnish with whole berries and rose petals and serve immediately. Or cover loosely and refrigerate for up to several hours; garnish just before serving.

Makes 6 servings.

VARIATIONS: Omit the berries and rose water or syrup. Peel and pit about 3 pounds ripe soft fruit such as apricots, figs, mangoes, nectarines, or peaches. Coarsely purée the pulp, sweeten to taste with sugar and freshly squeezed lemon or lime juice, chill, and fold into the whipped cream. Or cook rhubarb or gooseberries until tender, then purée, sweeten to taste, chill, and fold into the cream.

4 cups ripe berries
Granulated sugar
2 cups heavy (whipping) cream, well chilled
3 tablespoons powdered sugar
Rose water or rose syrup
Whole ripe fresh berries for garnish
Pesticide-free rose petals for garnish

Old South Fromage

2½ cups water
1½ envelopes (scant 1½ tablespoons)
  unflavored gelatin
1 cup sugar
4 small oranges
1 cup freshly squeezed orange juice
½ cup freshly squeezed lemon juice
1 pound marshmallows, chopped
½ cup finely chopped pecans
1 cup heavy (whipping) cream, well
  chilled
Additional orange segments or
  candied orange zest for garnish
  (optional)
Pesticide-free gardenia for garnish
  (optional)
Whole fresh mint leaves for garnish

Georgia Taliaferro, a wonderful cook from my hometown of Jonesville, Louisiana, always made this dish for church "dinner-on-the-grounds," the large-scale potluck that followed morning services.

I'm not sure of the origin of the name fromage (pronounced "frummage" back home); perhaps it migrated to the Deep South from the French *fromage bavarois*, or "Bavarian cheese," used to describe a rich whipped froth that is similar in texture to a Bavarian cream. Instead of allowing the refreshingly light-yet-rich mixture to set in a mold, Georgia always used a beautiful bowl from which the fromage was directly served.

In a small bowl, combine ½ cup of the water and the gelatin and stir well. Set aside to soften for about 5 minutes.

In a saucepan, combine the sugar and the remaining 2 cups water. Place over high heat, bring to a boil, and cook, stirring occasionally, until the sugar dissolves, about 5 minutes. Remove from the heat and stir in the softened gelatin until the gelatin dissolves. Pour into a large serving bowl and let cool to room temperature.

Remove the peel, including all white pith, from the oranges. Cut the oranges into segments and remove all membrane encasing segments. Cut each segment in half crosswise. Add to the cooled gelatin mixture. Stir in the orange and lemon juices. Cover and refrigerate until the mixture begins to congeal, about 35 to 45 minutes.

In a chilled bowl, whip the cream until it forms soft peaks. Cover and refrigerate.

Remove the orange mixture from the refrigerator. Fold in the marshmallows, pecans, and whipped cream, incorporating well. Transfer to a serving bowl, cover and refrigerate for 24 hours.

Garnish the fromage with orange segments or zest (if used) or a gardenia (if used) and/or mint leaves. Spoon from the bowl at the table.

Makes 8 to 10 servings.

PUDDINGS

Here are the sticky, gooey cakelike puddings that warm our souls. Dark, rich persimmon pudding is my preferred cool-weather dessert; I squirrel away frozen persimmon purée during the brief persimmon season for winter-long bakings. Bread pudding takes me back to my years in New Orleans and is always a crowd pleaser, whether I serve it for breakfast, coffee break, afternoon snack, or dessert.

Pudding cakes, also known as sponge puddings, surprise puddings, or soufflé puddings, miraculously separate during baking into a layer of sponge cake on top of a sauce.

English heritage puddings such as queen of puddings, cabinet pudding, and spotted dick deserve a new look. Steamed puddings are a British legacy from the days of Henry VIII, and although they enjoy a reputation of being complicated desserts, they are really very easy to prepare and can be made ahead and reheated.

I've also included one of the few Asian puddings that I know. It is a thick stove-top blend of rice and carrots, exotically perfumed with rose water and showered in edible gold or silver leaf.

STEAMING

Use a steamer with a rack or insert a rack, tart ring, or other device into a large pot that will lift the pudding container about 2 inches above the bottom of the pot and will allow steam to circulate around the pudding container. Pour in enough boiling water so that the bottom of the pudding mold will rest just above the water line. Position the tightly covered pudding mold on the rack over the gently boiling water and tightly cover the pot. To ensure that the pudding will rise properly, adjust the heat and add more boiling water as necessary throughout cooking in order to maintain the original water level and a continual gentle boil.

STORING

Persimmon pudding, bread pudding, and other cakelike puddings are best eaten still warm from the oven. Leftovers can be refrigerated and reheated in a microwave or in a slow oven.

Moist steamed puddings such as the Steamed Plum Pudding on page 86 can be stored for up to 3 months. Cool the unmolded pudding to room temperature. Meanwhile, soak several layers of cheesecloth in rum or brandy. Wrap the pudding in the cheesecloth to cover well, then wrap tightly in plastic wrap or aluminum foil. Store in a cool, dry place. Unwrap occasionally and add more rum or brandy if the pudding seems dry.

Baked Persimmon Pudding

I normally offer both Custard Cream (page 88) and Caramel Sauce (page 89) for pouring over this moist dessert; diners may choose either or use both in combination. For an elegant presentation, ladle one of the sauces onto each large plate and top with a scoop of the pudding, then dribble small pools of the other sauce on top of the first sauce and pull a wooden skewer through the sauces to create a pattern. Good sauce alternatives include Hard Sauce (page 90), Whipped Cream (page 91), or rich vanilla ice cream.

Alternatively, the mixture can be spooned into a 2-quart pudding mold and steamed according to the directions on page 85.

Preheat an oven to 350° F. Butter a shallow 9-inch square or round baking dish.

In a bowl, combine the flour, baking powder, baking soda, salt, cinnamon, and ginger. Stir to mix thoroughly; set aside.

In the bowl of an electric mixer, combine the eggs and sugar. Beat until well blended. Stir in the melted butter and vanilla or rum. Add the dry ingredients and stir until moistened. Slowly stir in the half-and-half and persimmon purée. Mix in the raisins and pecans. Pour into the prepared baking dish.

Transfer the dish to a large baking pan, place the pan in the oven, and pour in enough hot water (not boiling) to reach about halfway up the sides of the baking dish. Bake until a slender, wooden skewer inserted into the center comes out almost clean, about 1½ hours. Transfer to a wire rack and let cool slightly.

Serve warm with selected sauce (see recipe introduction).

Makes 8 servings.

Softened unsalted butter for greasing baking dish
2 cups all-purpose flour
1 teaspoon baking powder
1 teaspoon baking soda
½ teaspoon salt
1½ teaspoons ground cinnamon
1 teaspoon ground ginger
3 eggs
1½ cups granulated or firmly packed light brown sugar
½ cup (1 stick) unsalted butter, melted and cooled
1 tablespoon pure vanilla extract, or 2 tablespoons rum
2 cups half-and-half
2 cups persimmon purée (from 5 or 6 very ripe persimmons)
1 cup raisins
1 cup chopped pecans or other nuts

Indian Carrot Pudding
(Cajar ki Kheer)

4 cups milk
2 tablespoons basmati or other long-
    grain white rice
1 pound carrots, peeled and finely
    grated or chopped
⅓ cup sugar
¼ cup chopped blanched pistachios
    or blanched almonds
¼ teaspoon ground cardamom
About ¼ cup heavy (whipping) cream
    or freshly made or canned
    coconut milk
1 teaspoon rose water, or to taste
Silver leaf and/or gold leaf slivers for
    garnish (optional)

In India, puddings like this are adorned for special occasions with slivers of tissue-thin silver leaf or gold leaf. These inert metals are edible and may be purchased at art-supply stores and some fancy-food shops.

In a heavy saucepan, place the milk over medium-high heat and bring to a boil. Sprinkle the rice into the boiling milk, stirring constantly for several minutes to keep the rice from settling on the pan bottom. Reduce the heat to medium-low and cook the rice at a gentle boil until the milk is reduced by half and the rice is tender, about 20 minutes, stirring often to prevent a skin from forming on the surface of the milk.

Stir the carrots into the milk-rice mixture and continue cooking until the carrots are tender and the mixture is reduced to a thick sauce, about 15 minutes; stir frequently to prevent scorching on the bottom.

Stir the sugar, about two thirds of the pistachios or almonds, and the cardamom into the pudding and cook, stirring constantly, until the mixture begins to stick to the pan bottom, about 10 minutes. Remove from the heat, spoon into a bowl, and let cool to room temperature.

Stir ¼ cup of the cream or coconut milk and the rose water into the pudding. Cover tightly with plastic wrap or aluminum foil and chill for at least 3 hours.

Shortly before serving, remove from the refrigerator and check consistency; it should be a bit thinner than traditional rice pudding. If it seems too thick, stir in a little more cream or coconut milk. Spoon into individual bowls and sprinkle with the remaining pistachios and the silver and/or gold (if used).

Makes 6 servings.

Maple Sponge Pudding Cake

Canadian food writer Anita Stewart shared this recipe that she gathered at L'Escapade, an inn at Mont Tremblant, Quebec. With a few modifications, it has become one of my standby quick-and-easy desserts. The sauce poured over the top ends up on the bottom.

Preheat an oven to 350° F. Butter a 2-quart glass casserole or other baking dish.

In a bowl, combine the sugar, flour, baking powder, and salt and stir to mix well. Whisk in the milk and ¼ cup of the butter to blend well. Scrape the fairly stiff batter into the prepared baking dish.

In a saucepan, bring the syrup to a boil. Remove from the heat and stir in the remaining ¼ cup butter and the vanilla. Immediately pour the mixture over the pudding batter. Bake until puffy, bubbling, and golden brown, 35 to 45 minutes.

Serve warm. Offer crème fraîche or a pitcher of cream for topping the pudding at the table.

Makes 6 servings.

CHOCOLATE VARIATION: Add 6 tablespoons unsweetened cocoa powder, preferably Dutch-process type, to the flour mixture. Slowly stir 6 tablespoons unsweetened cocoa powder into the syrup before heating.

Softened unsalted butter for greasing baking dish
¾ cup sugar
2 cups all-purpose flour, preferably unbleached
2 teaspoons baking powder
Pinch of salt
1 cup milk
½ cup (1 stick) unsalted butter, melted and cooled
1 cup maple syrup
1 teaspoon pure vanilla extract
Crème fraîche or heavy (whipping) cream for topping

Lemon Sponge Pudding Cake

Softened unsalted butter for greasing
  baking pan or dish
1 cup sugar
¼ cup (½ stick) unsalted butter,
  softened
2 teaspoons finely grated or minced
  lemon zest, preferably from
  Meyer lemons
3 eggs, separated
¼ cup all-purpose flour, preferably
  unbleached
Pinch of salt
1¼ cups milk
½ cup freshly squeezed lemon juice,
  preferably from Meyer lemons
Fresh berries or Fresh Berry Sauce
  (page 90)

Here's another old-time pudding cake that separates during baking into spongy cake crowning a creamy sauce. Some people like to serve this chilled, but I only like it warm from the oven.

Preheat an oven to 350° F. Butter an 8-inch square baking pan or a 1½-quart baking dish.

In the bowl of an electric mixer, combine the sugar, butter, and lemon zest. Beat until fluffy, about 3 minutes. Add the egg yolks, one at a time, beating well after each addition. Stir in the flour, salt, milk, and lemon juice. Set aside.

In a separate bowl, beat the egg whites until they form stiff, shiny peaks but are not dry. Stir about one fourth of the whites into the batter to lighten it. Using a rubber spatula, fold in the remaining whites. Pour the mixture into the prepared baking container.

Transfer the baking pan or dish to a baking pan, place the pan in the oven, and pour in enough hot (not boiling) water to reach about halfway up the sides of the pudding container. Bake until the top pudding layer is set and lightly browned, about 45 minutes.

Serve warm with berries or offer Fresh Berry Sauce.

Makes 4 to 6 servings.

VARIATIONS: Substitute juice and zest of lime, orange, tangerine, or grapefruit for the lemon, or use a combination of citrus.

For pineapple sponge pudding, reduce the sugar to ¾ cup and the milk to ¾ cup. Add 1 cup pineapple juice along with the milk. Omit the lemon juice and zest.

Creole Bread Pudding

Years ago when I lived in the French Quarter, I frequently enjoyed this treat at the Coffee Pot, where Pearl made it every day. Before leaving New Orleans, I talked her out of the recipe, which has been a standby in my kitchen ever since.

To make the pudding, in a bowl, combine the eggs, granulated sugar, milk, cream, butter, vanilla and almond extracts, currants or raisins, and nutmeg; whisk to blend well. Place the bread slices in a large bowl, pour the egg mixture over the top, and let stand, turning bread as necessary, until the bread is soft and saturated with the custard mixture, about 30 minutes.

Arrange the bread slices in 2 layers in a lightly greased 8-inch square or round baking dish and pour any unabsorbed custard mixture over the top of the bread. Cover and refrigerate for at least 3 hours or as long as overnight.

Preheat an oven to 350° F.

Bake until the custard is set and the top is lightly browned, about 45 minutes. During baking, occasionally push the bread down into the sauce with the back of a wooden spoon.

Meanwhile, prepare the sauce. If necessary, reheat just before serving.

To serve, dust the top of the pudding with powdered sugar. Spoon the warm pudding into shallow bowls and ladle some of the sauce over the top.

Makes 6 servings.

2 eggs
¾ cup granulated sugar
3 cups milk
1 cup heavy (whipping) cream
½ cup (1 stick) unsalted butter, melted
2 teaspoons pure vanilla extract
1 teaspoon almond extract
½ cup dried currants or raisins
1 teaspoon freshly grated nutmeg, or to taste
8 ounces (½ loaf) stale French bread, sliced ½ inch thick
Warm Liquor Sauce (page 90), made with bourbon or Southern Comfort liqueur
Powdered sugar for dusting

BREAD PUDDING VARIATIONS

Follow the directions for assembling the bread pudding on the preceding page, using one of the suggested variations.

Banana Bread Pudding. Make or purchase banana bread to replace the French bread. Substitute chopped crystallized ginger for the currants or raisins. Serve with Custard Cream (page 88) or Whipped Cream (page 91).

Bread Loaf Pudding. Use a long loaf of thinly sliced white sandwich bread instead of the French bread. Cut off and discard the crusts and trim the slices so that they stand upright in a buttered 9-by-5-inch loaf pan. Omit the currants or raisins. Dip the bread slices into the custard, then pack the slices rather tightly in the pan to resemble a loaf of bread. Pour the remaining custard over the bread, cover tightly, and refrigerate overnight before baking. After baking, cool to room temperature, then chill the loaf overnight. Turn out of the pan and slice the pudding crosswise. Ladle Custard Cream (page 88) onto individual plates, then fan out 3 slices of the pudding on top.

Chocolate Bread Pudding. Use day-old chocolate pound cake instead of the French bread. Omit the currants or raisins. Add 1 cup chopped pecans to the custard mixture. Serve warm with warm Chocolate Sauce (page 88) or Custard Cream (page 88).

Chocolate-Caramel Bread Pudding. This variation was inspired by a dessert that I devoured at Mark Miller's Coyote Cafe in Santa Fe. Use day-old chocolate pound cake instead of the French bread. Reduce the sugar to ⅓ cup and substitute 1 cup Caramelized Goat's Milk Sauce *(Cajeta)* on page 89 or Caramel Sauce (page 89) for the cream. Omit the currants or raisins. Add 1 cup toasted pine nuts to the custard mixture. Serve with both Chocolate Sauce (page 88) and Caramelized Goat's Milk Sauce (page 89) or Caramel Sauce (page 89).

Croissant Bread Pudding. Use stale croissants, sliced horizontally, in place of the French bread. Substitute golden raisins or chopped candied orange zest for the currants or raisins.

Date-Nut Bread Pudding. Omit the currants or raisins. Add 1 cup chopped pitted dates and 1 cup chopped pecans or other nuts to the custard mixture. Serve with Lemon Sauce (page 89).

Gingerbread Pudding. Bake your favorite gingerbread (I prefer Moosehead Gingerbread from *The Fannie Farmer Baking Book* by Marion Cunningham) to use in place of the French bread. When the gingerbread is very cold, slice it and lightly toast the slices in the oven to dry them. Serve warm with Old-fashioned Pudding Sauce (page 90) or Lemon Sauce (page 89).

Pumpkin Bread Pudding. Make or purchase pumpkin bread to replace the French bread. Sweeten the custard with maple syrup or golden brown sugar instead of the granulated sugar. Use chopped dried dates in place of the currants or raisins. When the pudding comes out of the oven, pour warm Caramel Sauce (page 89) over the top; let stand for a few minutes before serving.

Mexican Bread and Cheese Pudding (*Capirotada*)

1 Mexican raw sugar cone (*piloncillo*), or 1 cup firmly packed dark brown sugar or granulated raw sugar
2 cups water
5 cups cubed or torn bite-sized pieces stale hard rolls or French bread
1 cup freshly squeezed orange juice
One 5-inch cinnamon stick
3 or 4 whole cloves
1 cup raisins
1 cup milk, light cream, or half-and-half
¼ cup (½ stick) unsalted butter, melted
2½ cups freshly shredded medium-sharp Cheddar cheese
1 cup pine nuts or chopped almonds, peanuts, or other nuts
Whipped Cream (page 91) for topping (optional)

Some cooks in both Old and New Mexico make this yummy tradition even richer by using stale pound cake in place of the bread.

Several hours before making the pudding, place the sugar cone in a bowl and cover with the water. If using light brown or granulated raw sugar, reserve.

Preheat an oven to 350° F. Butter a 1½-quart baking dish, preferably made of earthenware.

Spread the bread in a single layer on a baking sheet and toast in the oven until golden brown, 10 to 20 minutes. Transfer to a large bowl.

In a saucepan, combine the piloncillo sugar (if used) dissolved in the water, orange juice, cinnamon, cloves, and raisins; if using brown or granulated raw sugar, add it and the 2 cups water. Bring to a boil over medium-high heat and cook, stirring, until the sugar dissolves. Remove from the heat. Discard the cinnamon stick and cloves, if desired. Stir in the milk, light cream, or half-and-half and butter until well mixed.

Pour over the bread and toss well. Add 2 cups of the cheese and ¾ cup of the nuts. Toss to mix well.

Turn the bread mixture into the prepared baking dish. Sprinkle with the remaining cheese and nuts. Cover with a lid or aluminum foil and bake until most of the liquid is absorbed and the pudding is set, about 1 hour; uncover occasionally and push down on the top with the back of a wooden spoon to immerse the bread in the syrup.

Remove the pudding to a wire rack to cool. Serve warm, at room temperature, or cover and chill for several hours or overnight. If desired, serve with whipped cream.

Makes 6 servings.

APPLE OR PEAR VARIATION: Add about 3 cups peeled, cored, and thinly sliced apple or pear with the 2 cups cheese.

Queen of Puddings

Leave it to the British to elevate a lowly bread-crumb pudding to royal status with a crown of meringue.

Butter an 8- or 9-inch round shallow pan. Spread a thin layer of the jam, marmalade, curd, or fruit purée in the bottom of the pan. Set aside.

In a heavy saucepan, place the milk over medium-low heat until bubbles form along the edges of the pan. Remove from the heat and set aside to cool slightly.

In a bowl, combine the bread crumbs, lemon zest, butter, and ¼ cup of the sugar. In a small bowl, lightly whisk the egg yolks and add to the mixture. Stir in the milk until all the ingredients are well mixed. Stir in the vanilla. Pour into the prepared baking dish and let stand for about 30 minutes to soften the bread crumbs.

Preheat an oven to 350° F.

Transfer the baking dish to a large baking pan, place the pan in the oven, and pour in enough hot (not boiling) water to reach about halfway up the sides of the pudding dish. Bake until the pudding is set and a knife inserted near the edge comes out barely clean, about 40 minutes. Remove from the oven and set aside to cool slightly. Leave the oven on.

In the bowl of an electric mixer, combine the egg whites and cream of tartar. Beat until they form soft peaks. Continuing to beat, gradually sprinkle in the remaining 3 tablespoons sugar until the whites form stiff, shiny peaks but are not dry.

Spread a thin layer of jam, marmalade, curd, or fruit purée over the custard. Using a pastry bag fitted with a plain or fluted tip, pipe the egg whites in peaks around the top edge of the pudding. Alternatively, form the peaks with a spoon. Top each peak with a candied fruit (if used). Bake until lightly browned, about 8 minutes. Serve warm.

Makes 4 servings.

About ½ cup apricot or berry jam, orange or ginger marmalade, orange or lemon curd (homemade, page 92, or purchased) or puréed fruit
2 cups milk
1 cup fine fresh breadcrumbs or crumbled cake or sugar cookies
Zest of 1 lemon
2 tablespoons unsalted butter, melted and cooled
¼ cup plus 3 tablespoons sugar, preferably superfine
4 eggs, separated
1 teaspoon pure vanilla extract
¼ teaspoon cream of tartar
Candied apricots, cherries, or other fruits (optional)

Almond Cabinet Pudding

½ pound mixed dried fruit (about 2 cups)
3 cups milk
4 ounces (about 6 slices) pound cake, sponge cake, or bread (crusts discarded), sliced and cut into ½- to 1-inch squares
¾ cup crumbled *amaretti* or other almond macaroons
6 egg yolks
3 tablespoons sugar (if using cake), or 6 tablespoons sugar (if using bread)
1 teaspoon almond extract
Softened unsalted butter for greasing baking dish
Lemon Sauce (page 89) or Warm Liquor Sauce (page 90)

Here's another British tradition in which bread or cake is cooked in a custard mixture. It differs from American bread pudding in that it is encased within dried fruits and steamed instead of baked.

In a bowl, cover the dried fruit with hot water. Soak until softened, about 30 minutes.

Pour 2 cups of the milk into a heavy saucepan. Place over medium-low heat until bubbles form along the edges of the pan. Remove from the heat to cool slightly.

In a bowl, combine the cake or bread pieces and crumbled macaroons. Strain in the warm milk. Set aside for about 20 minutes.

In a separate bowl, combine the egg yolks and sugar and whisk until well blended. Whisk in the remaining 1 cup milk and the almond extract. Pour over the soaking bread and stir to combine.

Prepare a pot for steaming as described on page 63. Grease a 1½-quart soufflé dish or other baking dish with butter.

Drain the dried fruit, squeeze out excess moisture, and arrange the fruit on the bottom and sides of the buttered baking dish. Pour in the custard mixture. Cover tightly with aluminum foil. Place on the steamer rack over the gently boiling water, cover, and steam until set, about 2 hours; be sure that the water remains at a gentle boil and add additional boiling water if needed to maintain original level.

Prepare the sauce; set aside.

Transfer the steamed pudding to a wire rack, uncover, and let cool for 15 minutes.

To serve, run a knife around the edges of the pudding to loosen them, invert a large serving plate on top, and invert the pudding. Lift off the pudding mold. Gently reheat the sauce and ladle it around the edges of the pudding.

Makes 6 to 8 servings.

Spotted Dick

1 cup all-purpose flour
2 teaspoons baking powder
3 tablespoons granulated sugar
Pinch of salt
½ cup chopped suet, or ½ cup (1
    stick) unsalted butter, cut into
    small pieces
1 cup dried currants or raisins
About ⅓ cup milk
Lemon Sauce (page 89), Old-
    fashioned Pudding Sauce (page
    90), or Custard Cream (page 88)
Powdered sugar for dusting

Also known as plum bolster, this venerable English pudding is traditionally boiled inside a pudding cloth. The first pudding known to have been boiled in this manner was served at Cambridge University in the seventeenth century.

When chopped dried fruit is substituted for the currants or raisins, the pudding is dubbed spotted dog; when the plain dough is rolled out, spread with jam, and rolled up jelly-roll fashion, the pudding is called jam roly-poly.

In a pot about 10 inches in diameter, pour water to a depth of about 4 inches. Bring to a boil.

Meanwhile, in a bowl, combine the flour, baking powder, granulated sugar, and salt and stir to mix well. Add the suet or butter, currants or raisins, and just enough milk or water to form a fairly stiff dough. Turn the dough out onto a floured work surface and roll with the palms of your hands into a log shape, 1½ to 2 inches in diameter. Wrap loosely in waxed paper or parchment paper, then wrap loosely in a clean damp cloth dusted with flour or in foil; do not wrap too tightly to allow room for expansion. Tie cloth with cotton string or twist ends of foil to seal.

Place the roll so that it lies flat in the boiling water, cover, and adjust heat to maintain a slow boil. Cook until set, about 2 hours, adding more boiling water as necessary to maintain original level.

Meanwhile, prepare the selected sauce.

Remove the wrapped pudding to a wire rack to drain briefly. Unwrap and place on a serving plate. Sprinkle with powdered sugar.

To serve, slice crosswise into 4 to 6 equal pieces. Serve warm with sauce.

Makes 4 to 6 servings.

Steamed Ginger Pudding

Ginger in three forms adds a special flavor to this English-style pudding.

If you don't have a pudding mold with a clamp-down lid, choose a tin mold such as a charlotte pan or even a clean coffee can. After pouring the pudding mixture into the pan, cover the top with a double layer of heavy-duty aluminum foil, then tie the foil tightly in place with cotton string or seal it with duct tape.

Serve the pudding warm with softly whipped cream, ice cream, or Custard Cream (page 88) made with orange zest.

Prepare a pot for steaming as described on page 63. Butter the insides and the inside of the lid of a 2- to 3-quart pudding mold with a tight-fitting lid. Dust with granulated sugar, shaking off excess. Set aside.

In a large mixing bowl, combine the butter or suet and brown sugar and mix until light and fluffy. Add the eggs, one at a time, beating well after each addition. Add the bread crumbs, flour, baking powder, salt, ginger root, ground ginger, nutmeg, cinnamon, orange and lemon zests, and vanilla, brandy, or liqueur; mix well. Fold in the raisins and crystallized or preserved ginger and pour into the prepared mold.

Cover the pudding mold tightly and place on the steamer rack over the gently boiling water, cover, and steam until the pudding pulls back slightly from the edges of the mold and a wooden skewer inserted into the center comes out almost clean, about 1½ hours; be sure that the water remains at a gentle boil and add additional boiling water if needed to maintain original level.

Transfer the mold to a wire rack to cool for about 10 minutes. Uncover the mold, invert a serving plate on top of the mold, and invert the mold. Lift off the mold. Lightly dust the pudding with powdered sugar; sprinkle with citrus zest and garnish with ginger strips.

Makes 8 servings.

Softened unsalted butter for greasing pudding mold
Granulated sugar for dusting mold
½ cup (1 stick) unsalted butter, at room temperature, or 3 ounces beef suet, chopped
1½ cups firmly packed golden brown sugar
4 eggs
1⅓ cups fine fresh white or whole-wheat bread crumbs
1½ cups all-purpose flour
1 teaspoon baking powder
1 teaspoon salt
2 tablespoons minced or grated fresh ginger root
2 teaspoons ground ginger
½ teaspoon freshly grated nutmeg
½ teaspoon ground cinnamon
2 tablespoons grated or minced orange zest
1 teaspoon grated or minced lemon zest
2 teaspoons pure vanilla extract, or ¼ cup brandy or ginger-flavored liqueur
1½ cups golden raisins
½ cup finely chopped crystallized or preserved ginger
Powdered sugar for dusting
Minced orange and lemon zest for garnish
Crystallized or preserved ginger, cut into julienne strips, for garnish

CASTLE PUDDINGS

In England, both towering puddings steamed in elaborate molds and individual steamed puddings are called castle puddings. Use the Ginger Steamed Pudding or any of the steamed puddings on this page. Or prepare either of the sponge pudding mixtures on pages 69 and 70. For individual puddings, divide the mixture evenly among timbales or other individual-sized molds, cover, and steam for 30 minutes to 1 hour.

FLAMING PUDDINGS

To flame a steamed pudding for a dramatic presentation, place the warm pudding on a serving plate. In a small saucepan over medium heat, warm about ½ cup rum or brandy. Rush the pan to the table. Ignite the rum or brandy with a long-handled match or lighter. Pour the flaming spirit over the pudding. After the flames subside, cut and serve the pudding.

Using the preceding recipe for Steamed Ginger Pudding as a guide, try the following variations on the theme. For the photograph, I made the Steamed Plum Pudding.

Steamed Cherry Pudding. Cream ½ cup (1 stick) unsalted butter with 1 cup sugar. Beat in 2 eggs. Combine 2½ cups all-purpose flour, 1 tablespoon baking powder, and a pinch of salt. Alternately add the dry ingredients and 1 cup milk to the egg mixture and stir until well blended. Stir in 2 cups pitted fresh, frozen, or drained canned cherries. Spoon into a buttered mold and steam as directed for 1½ hours. Serve with Old-fashioned Pudding Sauce (page 90).

Steamed Chocolate Pudding. Melt 3 ounces semisweet chocolate with ¼ cup (½ stick) unsalted butter. Combine with ½ cup firmly packed light brown sugar, 3 eggs, and 1 cup half-and-half. Stir in 1 cup all-purpose flour, 1 tablespoon instant-espresso powder, 1½ cups fine chocolate wafer crumbs, 1 tablespoon baking powder, ¼ teaspoon salt, and 1 teaspoon pure vanilla extract. Spoon into a buttered mold and steam as directed. Serve with Custard Cream or Chocolate Sauce (page 88).

Steamed Plum Pudding. In a bowl, combine 1 cup chopped mixed dried fruits (apples, apricots, peaches, pears), 1 cup chopped stewed pitted prunes, 1 cup grated fresh apple, 1 cup black raisins, 1 cup golden raisins, ½ cup dried currants, 2 tablespoons minced or grated orange zest, 1 tablespoon minced or grated lemon zest, 1 cup chopped nuts, ¼ cup freshly squeezed orange juice, and ⅓ cup rum or brandy. In a food processor, cream ½ cup (1 stick) butter with ¾ cup firmly packed dark brown sugar. Beat in 3 eggs, one at a time. Add 1 cup fine dried bread crumbs, ½ cup all-purpose flour, 1 teaspoon baking powder, 2 teaspoons ground cinnamon, 1 teaspoon freshly grated nutmeg, ½ teaspoon ground cloves, and ¼ teaspoon salt. Process until well mixed. Add ½ cup dark beer or milk and process until blended. Pour into the bowl holding the fruit-nut mixture and mix well. Spoon into a buttered mold and steam as directed for 4 hours. Serve with Hard Sauce (page 90).

FINISHING TOUCHES

Although most custards, mousses, and puddings are quite wonderful on their own, sometimes a ladleful of sauce, a crown of whipped cream or meringue, or a shower of a crunchy topping elevates them to an even higher ethereal status.

Custard Cream
(Crème Anglaise)

Use as a sauce for thick, rich puddings such as a stirred chocolate pudding, bread pudding, or persimmon pudding. Don't despair if the sauce is foamy at the beginning; it will turn out creamy.

2 cups milk
½ vanilla bean, split lengthwise, or 1
to 2 teaspoons pure vanilla extract
8 egg yolks, at room temperature
½ cup sugar

In a heavy saucepan, combine the milk and vanilla bean (if used). Place over medium-low heat and heat until bubbles form along the edges of the pan.

In the top pan of a double boiler, whisk or beat the egg yolks and sugar until pale yellow. Continuing to whisk, gradually add the hot milk; transfer the vanilla bean to the mixture. Place over barely simmering water and whisk just until the custard registers 170° to 175° F on a candy thermometer or thickens to the density of a creamy sauce, about 15 minutes; do not overcook or eggs may scramble. It should coat the back of a spoon, and your finger should leave a trail when you trace it across the spoon.

Strain the mixture through a fine-mesh sieve into a bowl. Stir in the vanilla extract to taste (if used). Cover with plastic wrap or waxed paper and press it directly onto the surface of the custard. Serve warm, at room temperature, or refrigerate until well chilled, as long as overnight. Remove the vanilla bean before serving.

Makes about 2 cups.

VARIATIONS: For a richer flavor, substitute heavy (whipping) cream or half-and-half for half of the milk. For a thinner, less rich sauce, reduce the number of egg yolks to 4 or 5.

For a delicate citrus flavor, add strips of lemon, orange, or other citrus zest to the milk before heating.

For a spirited flavor, omit the vanilla and stir in a favorite liqueur.

Chocolate Sauce

Instead of the vanilla, flavor the sauce with a liqueur such as Amaretto, Frangelico, or Kahlúa.

8 ounces semisweet or bittersweet
chocolate, finely chopped
2 tablespoons unsalted butter
1 cup heavy (whipping) cream
1 teaspoon pure vanilla extract

In a heavy saucepan, combine the chocolate, butter, and cream. Place over low heat and cook, stirring frequently, until the chocolate melts and the mixture is smooth. Stir in the vanilla extract and serve warm. If made ahead, cool to room temperature, then refrigerate; slowly reheat just to warm before serving.

Makes about 1½ cups.

Caramel Sauce

Divine over dense puddings such as any of the bread puddings (pages 72-75) or on top of Pots of Cream (page 15).

1 cup heavy (whipping) cream
2 cups sugar
2 tablespoons freshly squeezed lemon
juice
½ cup (1 stick) unsalted butter

In a heavy saucepan, heat the cream over medium-low heat until bubbles form along the edges of the pan. Keep warm.

In a heavy saucepan, combine the sugar and lemon juice and stir until well mixed. Cover the pot and place it over medium-high heat until the sugar melts and bubbles, about 4 minutes. Remove the cover and occasionally swirl the pan or stir the mixture until the syrup is a golden amber color, 5 to 8 minutes. While cooking, brush the sides of the pan with a wet brush just above the bubbling sugar to keep crystals from forming. Stirring constantly, slowly pour in the warm cream. Bring to a boil, continuing to stir constantly. Cook until slightly thickened, about 3 minutes.

Remove the sauce from the heat, add the butter, and stir until the butter melts and the sauce is smooth. Serve immediately or cool to room temperature. If made in advance, cool to room temperature, then cover tightly and refrigerate for up to 2 weeks; reheat over a pan of simmering water or in a microwave oven.

Makes about 2 cups.

Caramelized Goat's Milk Sauce *(Cajeta)*

Here's an easy version of a normally more time-consuming sweet that is a favorite throughout Mexico and the Southwest. It is enjoyed as a thin pudding on its own, as a flavoring for other desserts, or as a sauce.

2 cans (14 ounces *each*) evaporated
goat's milk
2 cans (12 ounces each) sweetened
condensed milk
6 tablespoons (¾ stick) unsalted butter

In a saucepan, combine the milks and butter. Place over medium-high heat and bring to a boil. Cook, stirring almost continuously, for 10 minutes. Reduce the heat to medium-low and cook, stirring constantly, until the sauce thickens and is a medium tan color, about 5 minutes longer.

Serve warm or cool to room temperature, cover, and refrigerate for up to 2 weeks. Reheat in a microwave, stirring several times, or in a saucepan over low heat, stirring almost continuously, until smooth and warm; stir in a little milk or cream if the mixture is too thick.

Makes about 3 cups.

Lemon Sauce

This sauce may be made ahead and served at room temperature or refrigerated and gently reheated before serving.

1 cup sugar
Pinch of salt
1½ tablespoons cornstarch
1 cup water, boiling
3 tablespoons unsalted butter
¼ cup freshly squeezed lemon juice
1 tablespoon minced or grated lemon
zest
1 drop yellow food coloring (optional)

In a saucepan, combine the sugar, salt, and cornstarch. Slowly stir in the boiling water, blending well. Place over low heat and cook, stirring constantly, until the sauce is clear and thickened, about 5 minutes.

Remove from the heat. Add the butter, lemon juice and zest, and food coloring (if used) and stir until the butter melts.

Makes about 1½ cups.

Warm Liquor Sauce

I make this sauce with Southern Comfort liqueur to serve over Creole Bread Pudding (page 72).

1 cup sugar
¼ cup (½ stick) unsalted butter
3 tablespoons light cream or half-and-half
1 egg yolk, lightly beaten
About ¼ cup bourbon, brandy, rum, or other favorite liquor or liqueur

In a heavy saucepan, combine the sugar, butter, and light cream or half-and-half. Place over low heat and cook, stirring frequently, until the sugar dissolves. Remove from the heat. In a small bowl, stir about ¼ cup of the hot sauce into the egg yolk. Whisk into the sauce until well blended. Cool for about 5 minutes, then stir in the chosen liquor to taste. Serve warm.

Makes about 1½ cups.

Old-fashioned Pudding Sauce

This dates from my childhood and is great over steamed puddings or other dense or cakelike puddings.

1 cup sugar
1 tablespoon cornstarch
1 cup milk
¼ cup (½ stick) unsalted butter
1 teaspoon pure vanilla extract

In a small saucepan, combine the sugar and cornstarch and blend well. Slowly add the milk, stirring until smooth. Bring to a boil over medium-high heat and cook, stirring almost constantly, until the sauce is clear and thickened. Remove from the heat. Add the butter and vanilla and stir until the butter melts. Serve warm or at room temperature.

Makes about 1 cup.

Fresh Berry Sauce

Choose blackberries, blueberries, raspberries, strawberries, or other berries to make this simple topping.

4 cups fresh berries
2 to 3 tablespoons sugar, or to taste
1 tablespoon freshly squeezed lemon juice, kirsch, or framboise

In a food processor or blender, purée the berries. Pass through a fine-mesh sieve set over a bowl to remove seeds, if desired. Add the sugar and lemon juice or liqueur to taste.

Makes about 2 cups.

Hard Sauce

Traditional with steamed puddings, this warhorse is also good with persimmon pudding or bread puddings. Be sure that the pudding is hot so that the sauce melts onto it.

½ cup (1 stick) unsalted butter, at room temperature
1 cup powdered sugar
Pinch of salt
1 tablespoon pure vanilla extract, brandy, Cognac, or rum
About 3 tablespoons heavy (whipping) cream

In a bowl, cream the butter until light and fluffy. Gradually beat in the sugar and then the salt until well incorporated. Add the vanilla or spirits and enough cream to achieve a smooth, fluffy consistency. Cover and chill at least 3 hours. Let stand at room temperature for about 30 minutes before serving.

Makes about 1 cup.

Whipped Cream

For topping a pudding or folding into a Bavarian cream, whip cream just until it holds its shape; this is known as *crème chantilly*. For folding into a mousse, whip the cream a little stiffer, but avoid overbeating. The cornstarch present in powdered sugar helps stabilize whipped cream when liqueur or other liquids are added to it.

1 cup heavy (whipping) cream (not
    ultrapasteurized), well chilled
About 2 tablespoons granulated sugar,
    preferably superfine, or powdered
    sugar
½ teaspoon pure vanilla extract, or
    2 teaspoons liqueur or other spirits
    or cooled melted chocolate, or
    puréed fruits or fruit syrup to taste

Place a metal bowl and a wire whisk or the beaters of a hand-held mixer in the freezer until well chilled.

Pour the cream into the chilled bowl. Beat with the whisk or mixer just until the cream begins to thicken. Add the sugar and vanilla or other flavoring and continue to beat to the desired stage. Be very careful not to overbeat when using a mixer.

Makes about 2 cups.

Meringue Topping

This topping contains cream of tartar to stabilize the meringue, so do not beat the egg whites in a copper-lined bowl or the chemical reaction will turn the egg white greenish. An aluminum bowl will turn the mixture gray.

⅔ cup egg whites (about 5 eggs)
½ teaspoon cream of tartar
Pinch of salt
½ cup sugar, preferably superfine
1 teaspoon pure vanilla extract

Preheat an oven to 350° F.

Place the egg whites in a stainless-steel bowl set over simmering water and heat until warm to the touch. Beat until foamy. Add the cream of tartar and salt and continue beating until the whites form soft peaks. Add the sugar, 1 tablespoon at a time, beating well after each addition. Beat in the vanilla and continue to beat until the whites form stiff, shiny peaks but are not dry. Spread the meringue over the cooked pudding, making sure the meringue touches the inner edge of the pudding dish to prevent weeping and shrinkage. Using a spatula or knife blade, swirl the top of the egg whites decoratively. Bake until lightly browned, about 10 minutes.

To prevent shrinkage of the baked meringue, transfer the pudding to a draft-free place that is not too cold and let stand until serving time. Do not refrigerate.

Makes enough to cover one 9-inch round pudding or 6 individual puddings.

Chocolate Glaze

Instead of piping as directed, the glaze may be spooned to form a thin layer over baked custards.

8 ounces bittersweet or semisweet
    chocolate, finely chopped
¼ cup heavy (whipping) cream
3 tablespoons unsalted butter

In a microwave-safe bowl, combine the chocolate and cream and heat in a microwave oven at half power, stirring 2 or 3 times, until the chocolate melts. Alternatively, set the bowl in a pan of barely simmering water and stir gently until the chocolate melts and is smooth. Remove from the microwave or heat and gently whisk in the butter until melted.

Cool slightly, then transfer to a pastry bag fitted with a small plain tip or to a plastic bag with a tiny hole cut in one corner. Pipe the glaze over the chilled custards in desired pattern. Let stand until set.

Makes about 1 cup.

Lemon Curd

This tangy spread makes an excellent addition to English trifle. It is also good folded into whipped cream or crème fraîche as a pudding topping. Or stir it into plain stirred custard for a delicious lemon pudding. The curd keeps in the refrigerator for several weeks.

2 cups sugar, or to taste
Pinch of salt
5 egg yolks
3 whole eggs
1 cup freshly squeezed lemon juice
5 tablespoons unsalted butter

In a mixing bowl, stir together the sugar and salt. Add the egg yolks and whole eggs, one at a time, beating well after each addition. Stir in the lemon juice, then pour the mixture into the top pan of a double boiler set over simmering water. Add the butter, 1 tablespoon at a time, stirring constantly until the butter melts. When the mixture is thick enough to coat the back of a metal spoon, remove from the heat and cool completely before using. Cover and refrigerate.

Makes about 3 cups.

Chocolate Containers or Chocolate Leaves

Serve mousses or creamy puddings in edible chocolate containers. Choose small paper bags, paper muffin-tin liners, or small paper boxes to use as the molds. Or create your own molds by folding and taping together waxed paper or parchment paper in interesting shapes, such as the triangles shown on page 51.

For molding chocolate leaves, choose pesticide-free, nontoxic leaves such as camellia, citrus, mint, or roses.

½ pound high-quality milk, semisweet, bittersweet, or white chocolate containing cocoa butter, coarsely chopped

Line a baking sheet or tray with aluminum foil, parchment paper, or waxed paper; set aside.

Place the chocolate in a heatproof bowl. Set in a pan of barely simmering water and heat gently, stirring frequently, until the chocolate melts and is smooth. Alternatively, place the chocolate in a microwave-safe container and heat in a microwave oven at half power for semisweet or bittersweet chocolate or 30 percent power for milk or white chocolate, stirring 2 or 3 times, until the chocolate melts and is smooth.

To make chocolate containers, dip a pastry brush or soft paint brush into the chocolate and paint the inside of the paper mold to cover completely. Transfer to the lined baking sheet and refrigerate until firm, at least several hours or overnight; if stored overnight, cover the containers as soon as the chocolate is set.

To make chocolate leaves, dip a pastry brush or soft paint brush into the melted chocolate and paint the underside of the leaves; avoid painting the edges of the leaves. Chill as directed above.

Remove firm containers or leaves from the refrigerator, one at a time, and carefully peel off the paper or leaves. Seal the chocolate containers or leaves in plastic bags and refrigerate until serving time.

Makes 6 individual containers or about 18 leaves.

Crisp Cookie Cups

Bend the soft cookies into edible pudding bowls while still warm.

Softened unsalted butter for greasing baking sheet
2 egg whites, lightly beaten
½ cup sugar
½ cup finely chopped almonds, pine nuts, or other nuts
⅓ cup all-purpose flour
4 tablespoons (½ stick) unsalted butter, melted and cooled
¼ teaspoon almond extract

Preheat an oven to 400° F. Butter a baking sheet. Set aside several soup bowls that measure about 4 inches in diameter.

In a bowl, combine all ingredients and stir until smooth. Spoon the batter onto the prepared baking sheets to form dollops that are about 3 inches in diameter; make only as many cookies at a time as you have bowls ready. Using the back of a spoon, spread the batter out so that each cookie is about 5 inches in diameter and less than ¼ inch thick. Bake until browned around the edges, 6 to 8 minutes.

Using a spatula, carefully lift the warm cookies off the baking sheet. Transfer each cookie to a reserved bowl and mold the cookie to the bowl to form a cup, overlapping the edges slightly. Cool completely, then remove from the bowl.

Makes about 8 cookie cups.

Glazed Spiced Nuts

Crumble these crispy nuts over a smooth custard for a bit of crunch.

2 tablespoons unsalted butter
2 teaspoons ground cinnamon
1 cup pecans, walnuts, macadamia, or other nuts
¼ cup sugar

In a heavy sauté pan or skillet, melt the butter over medium-low heat. Add the cinnamon and nuts and toss to coat all over. Stir in the sugar and sauté until the sugar caramelizes and the nuts are crisp, about 5 minutes.

Pour onto a plate to cool.

Store in an airtight container for up to 1 week.

Makes 1 cup.

Praline Topping

Use as an alternative to caramelized sugar on créme brûlée or sprinkle over any custard for a bit of crunch. Choose your favorite nut or use a combination.

1½ cups sugar
½ cup water
Pinch of cream of tartar
1¾ cups nuts (about 6 ounces), coarsely chopped

Butter a baking sheet; set aside.

In a saucepan, combine the sugar and water and stir to mix well. Place over low heat and heat, without stirring, until the sugar dissolves. Stir in the cream of tartar. Increase the heat to high and cook until the syrup registers 330° F on a candy thermometer and is a rich amber color. Quickly stir in the nuts and pour onto the prepared baking sheet, spreading evenly. Set aside until cold and hard.

Lift the baking sheet and drop it onto a countertop to break up the praline. Using a rolling pin, crush the praline into crumbs, or grind in a food processor with on-off pulses until fine.

Store in an airtight container in a cool, dry place for up to 1 week.

Makes about 2 cups.

INDEX

INDEX TO PUDDINGS IN OTHER JAMES McNAIR COOKBOOKS

ACKNOWLEDGMENTS

Dishes have been graciously provided by the following stores: Fillamento, San Francisco, pages 14, 18, 23, 33, 48, 58, 68, 81, and 84; and Tántau, St. Helena, pages 26 and 45. Fabrics on pages 14, 56, and 72 are from Fillamento and on pages 17, 29, and 71 are from Tántau. Brass spoon on page 14 is from Fillamento.

Recipes were tested by: Margie Allen, John Carr, Martha Casselman, Chris Cook, Ruth Dosher, Jan Ellis, Carol Gallagher, Naila Gallagher, Vi Gianaras, Mary Ann Gilderbloom, Mark Gullikson, Gail High, Steven Holden, Marian May, Meri McEneny, Scottie McKinney, Lucille McNair, Martha McNair, Maile Moore, Sandra Moore, Jack Porter, John Richardson, Nancy and Tom Riess, Julie Schaper, Susannah Scher, Alice Russell-Shapiro, Michele Sordi, Brooksley Spence, Kristi Spence, Sara and Brad Timpson, and Sharon Woo.

To Marian May for sharing her idea for this book with me several years ago and for her excellent research and suggestions.

To Chronicle Books for finally agreeing to publish this book that I so passionately wanted to do.

To Sharon Silva for her usual outstanding copyediting.

To Cleve Gallat at CTA Graphics for his perfect typography and pasteup.

To my family and friends who always stand by me during every crisis and rejoice in every triumph. Special thanks to John Carr, Martha and Devereux McNair, John Richardson, and Felix Wiench who looked after things and thereby made it possible for me to take a much-needed vacation after completing my first draft.

To Beauregard Ezekiel Valentine, Joshua J. Chew, Michael T. Wigglebutt, and Dweasel Pickle for their companionship and occasional taste-testing.

To Andrew Moore for his unsurpassed assistance, amazing energy, and absolute devotion.